HisTruth IsMarching On

ADVANCED STUDIES ON PROPHECY IN THE LIGHT OF HISTORY

By Ralph Woodrow

A complete catalog of other books and tapes may be obtained upon request. Write to:

Ralph Woodrow
Evangelistic Assn., Inc.
P.O. Box 21
Palm Springs, CA 92263-0021

**HIS TRUTH IS MARCHING ON—Advanced
Studies on Prophecy in the Light of History**

International Standard Book Number: 0-916938-03-04.
Library of Congress Catalog Card Number: 77-84543.

Ralph Woodrow Evangelistic Association, Inc.
P. O. Box 124, Riverside, CA 92502-0124.

CONTENTS

INTRODUCTION

FROM THE EARLIEST times, by various means and methods, attempts have been made to predict the future. Zodiac charts, crystal balls, Ouija boards, the flight of birds, and even the intestines of animals have been used!

Hepatoscopy, which means "the inspection of the liver," was an ancient custom used by the Babylonians. Believing the liver was the seat of life, they would use a sheep's liver to predict the outcome of battles. This practice is mentioned in Ezekiel 21:21: "For the king of Babylon stood at the parting of the way, at the head of the two ways, to use divination: he made his arrows bright, he consulted with images, he *looked in the liver.*"

Isaiah mentioned "the astrologers, the stargazers, the monthly prognosticators" (Isa. 47:13). There have been psychics such as Michel Nostradamus, Edgar Cayce, and Jeane Dixon who have made numerous predictions. Some believe the future can be determined by time-cycles or by the Great Pyramid in Egypt.

But as Christians, we have "a MORE SURE WORD OF PROPHECY" than any of these! "Knowing this first, that no prophecy of the SCRIPTURE is of any private interpretation, for the prophecy came not in old time by the will of man but holy men of God spoke as they were *moved by the Holy Ghost*" (2 Peter 1:19-21).

As Christians, the purpose of Bible prophecy is not merely to predict the future, but to glorify *Him* who said: "I have told you before it come to pass, that, *when it is come to pass,* you might *believe*" (John 14:29). "The testimony of Jesus is the spirit of prophecy" (Rev. 19:10).

Many of the prophecies of the Bible, as will be shown in this book, have already been *fulfilled*. For anyone to take these prophecies, ignore the historical fulfillment, and try to match them with modern news headlines is not sound. It does not glorify the Lord. The folly of this practice has been especially apparent when dates have been set. It is not uncommon to read a booklet claiming certain alarming things will happen "within the next five years"—only to discover from the copyright notice that it was written twenty years ago!

In the pages that follow, certain "future or fulfilled" questions are before us—questions about the coming of Elijah, the 144,000, Joel's prophecy, and Ezekiel 38. Does the expression "day of the Lord" always refer to the end-time? Did the promise given to Abraham that his descendants would become a great nation ever find fulfillment? Will Russia invade Israel in the near future? Will Christ pass through the East Gate of Jerusalem when he returns? Will Jerusalem become the world's center of worship and government capital in the age to come?

In the chapter "The Kingdom of God—Postponed or Present?" we consider the kingdom *postponement* teaching and its implications. This will lead us to another question—one which has been often debated over the centuries—the question of the *millennium*. We will take a close look at passages such as Zechariah 14 and Isaiah 2.

There are differences of opinion as to the proper interpretation of many of these prophecies. We believe such differences should be dealt with in friendly discussion, realizing that the love of God causes us to be considerate and tolerant regarding the opinions of other Christians. We can disagree without being disagreeable.

When all the evidence is in, we believe it will be clear that God does not walk *backwards,* but his truth is marching ON!

—**Ralph Woodrow**

Chapter 1

WHICH YEAR WILL CHRIST RETURN?

IT WAS THE night of October 30, 1938. Orson Wells—then 23 years old—presented on radio a dramatic account of an invasion from Mars, complete with "news" bulletins and "eye-witness reports" about the invasion and accompanying destruction of the eastern portion of the United States!

Though an effort had been made to explain it was only a play, out of six million who heard the network program, it has been estimated that 2 million believed it was actually happening! Police headquarters, newspapers, and radio stations, were swamped with anguished calls. A young man in New Jersey went speeding to a priest so he could make "peace with God before dying." At 80 miles an hour, his car went out of control and overturned, but he escaped unhurt. It is said that two geology professors set out for New Jersey with the intention of buying the Martian cylinders to exhibit at their university!

Another time of mass fright followed September 11, 1909 when Professor Wolf announced that Halley's Comet would brush the earth on the night of May 18, 1910, leaving death and destruction in its path. A number of astronomers agreed with Wolf's conclusions. One astronomer announced that the comet's tail was composed of deadly cyanogen gas. Some people packed the cracks of their windows with rags and old papers to keep out the poisonous fumes! Some bought tanks of oxygen. Others figured that if the end was at hand, they might as well have a good time and "live it up." Still others were fearful and prayed. But the night of May 18, 1910, came and went, and the hysteria was soon forgotten.

History has also recorded times of mass excitement in connection with dates that have been set for the coming of Christ and the end of the age. Jesus said: "BUT OF THAT DAY AND THAT HOUR KNOWETH NO MAN, no not the angels

1

which are in heaven, neither the Son, but the Father. Take heed, watch and pray, for you know not when the TIME is" (Mk. 13:32,33; Matt. 24:36; 25:13). Nevertheless, over the centuries men have repeatedly set dates for this event. Some have sought to justify this by saying that we may not know "the day or hour"—but this does not mean we can't know the YEAR!

Thousands sincerely believed that Christ would return in the year 1844. William Miller—from whom the Adventists trace their beginning as a distinct movement—is generally credited (or discredited) with setting the 1844 date. When Miller first thought he knew when the Lord would return, he told only his wife and closest friends. For 13 years he remained silent on his farm. But he continued his study of the prophecies and attended church regularly. He was a Baptist.

Then one day in 1831, he was asked to come to a nearby town and share his ideas. This was the beginning. Being a farmer, the farmers and small town folks of New England in the 1830's felt this was a man they could trust. He was one of them. The word spread until thousands of Christians—scattered through various denominations—had accepted the Advent teaching and date of October 22, 1844.

When the day finally arrived, many gathered in churches and meeting halls to await the end. Others remained quietly at home. The daylight hours passed, then dusk and night. When the clock struck midnight, the failure of their hope was evident. An early Adventist wrote: "Such a spirit of weeping came over us as I never experienced before...we wept and wept till the day dawned."

The rumor still circulates that the Adventists dressed in white "ascension robes" and went out on hills to await the return of Christ. This charge is evidently untrue. Over many years a large reward was offered for proof of even *one* individual that did this. Surely, then, to give the impression that the whole Millerite movement did this in 1844 is misleading and unfair. They knew a robe made with their own hands could not be the robe of righteousness referred to in the Bible!

Miller believed the 1844 date was indicated by Daniel 8:14: "Unto two thousand and three hundred days; then shall the sanctuary be cleansed." Figuring that the 2300 days symbolized 2300 *years,* and that the prophecy should be measured from the same starting point as the 70 weeks (457 B.C.), he concluded that 2300 years would measure to the year 1844. The "sanctuary" he took to mean the earth; that it would be cleansed by the "flaming fire" that would accompany Christ at his coming.

It is difficult to understand how so many people became convinced that October 22, 1844 was the correct date, for the whole theory was based on assumptions, not plain statements: (1) It was assumed that the "sanctuary" meant the earth. (2) It was assumed that the "cleansing" of the sanctuary referred to the fire at Christ's return. (3) It was assumed that the 2300 days symbolized 2300 years. (4) It was assumed that the prophecy started at the same time as the 70 weeks prophecy, the latter being "cut off" from the former.

When Christ did not come at this time, some—including Miller—would not give up. They felt the 1844 date was correct! Hiram Edson, being disappointed along with the rest, advanced the teaching that Christ on this date cleansed the *heavenly* sanctuary, instead of the earth as they had supposed. This view was elaborated on by those who followed, especially by Mrs. Ellen G. White.

"In 1844, attended by heavenly angels," wrote Mrs. White, "our great High Priest entered the holy of holies, and there appears in the presence of God, to engage in the last acts of His ministration in behalf of man—to perform the work of investigative judgment, and to make atonement for all who are shown to be entitled to its benefits."[1]

Many feel this teaching—that Christ cleansed the heavenly sanctuary, began an investigative judgment, and made atonement in 1844—was formulated to justify the mistake about the 1844 date. I have a number of very fine neighbors and friends who are Adventists. I have no desire to discredit their sincerity and conviction, but do wonder why—after all these years—some still hold to the 1844 date.

To us, it is more feasible that Daniel's vision regarding the 2300 days had its fulfillment back within the Old Testament era. The kings that were symbolized in the vision by a two-horned ram and a goat with a horn between its eyes, were

3

ancient kings: "The ram which you saw having two horns are the kings of Media and Persia....And the rough goat is the king of Grecia [Greece]: and the great horn that is between his eyes is the first king" (Dan. 8:20, 21).

The first king of the Grecian empire was Alexander the Great. Later, he would be broken and "four kingdoms shall stand up" out of his kingdom (Dan. 8:8, 22). True to the prohecy, four kingdoms did emerge which were ruled over by Lysimachus, Cassander, Seleucus, and Ptolemy.

As the vision continued, Daniel saw the four horns of the goat "and out of one of them came forth a little horn, which waxed exceeding great...toward the pleasant land....Yea, he magnified himself even to [margin, against] the prince of the host, and by him the daily sacrifice was taken away, and the place of his sanctuary was cast down" (verses 9-11).

In short, this king who would rise out of one of the four parts into which the Grecian empire was divided, would destroy the holy people, would be powerful, would take away the daily sacrifice and defile the sanctuary—all of these things fit the career of the wicked Greek king Antiochus Epiphanes.

Albert Barnes has written: "All the circumstances of the prediction find a fulfillment in him, and if it were supposed that this was written after he had lived, and that it was the design of the writer to describe him by these symbols, he could not have found symbols that would have been more striking or appropriate than this."[2]

Antiochus resolved to exterminate the "holy people" utterly, and many of them were killed. Onias, the princely leader and high priest, was driven into exile and later was killed in a cruel manner. Stopping the worship of the Jews, the temple was dedicated to the pagan god Jupiter and became the scene of heathen revellings and orgies with harlots. Pigs were killed within the temple walls, their blood being poured over the furnishings of the holy place.

How long was this defilement of the sanctuary and the casting down of the holy people to continue? This brings us back to Daniel 8:14: "Unto two thousand and three hundred days; then shall the sanctuary be cleansed."

History has this to say about the cleansing of the sanctuary: "But Judas [Maccabee] and his brethren said, Behold, our enemies are discomfited: let us go up to cleanse the holy place, and to dedicate it afresh...and they went up unto mount Sion. And they saw the sanctuary laid desolate, and the altar profaned...and they rent their clothes, and made great lamentation...and they cleansed the holy place....And they took whole stones according to the law, and built a new altar after the fashion of the former...and offered sacrifice according to the law upon the new altar....And all the people fell upon their faces, and worshipped, and gave praise unto heaven, which had given them good success" (1 Maccabees, chapter 4). Thus was the sanctuary cleansed.

We believe that the total time of the persecution and defilement of the sanctuary was the period indicated by the prophecy—"two thousand and three hundred days." With all of the evidence pointing to a fulfillment within the Old Testament era, we see no reason to bypass this and seek a fulfillment in 1844.

Possibly some have minimized the historical fulfillment because of the wording: "at *the time of the end* shall be the vision" (Dan. 8:17). However, the vision deals with two kingdoms—both of which came to their "end" within the Old Testament period. The little horn (Antiochus Epiphanes) was to rise from one of the four parts of the Grecian empire "in the latter time of their kingdom" (verse 23). We conclude that the word "end" has to be understood within the time frame of the text.

We see no reason for stretching the 2300 days into 2300 years. We see no reason for applying the prophecy to a cleansing of the heavenly sanctuary in 1844. If the 2300 years began in 457 B.C. and ended in 1844 A.D., what happened in 457 B.C. to defile the heavenly sanctuary? Was a Greek king removed from the heavenly sanctuary in 1844?

ANOTHER FAMOUS DATE that was set for the second coming or presence of Christ and the end of Gentile rule was the year 1914. This was the date set by Charles Taze Russell who founded that movement which is today known as the Jehovah's Witnesses.

Writing 26 years before, Russell said that by 1914 "all present governments will be overthrown and dissolved"; that Jesus "will then be present as earth's new Ruler"; and that "neither Israel nor the world of mankind...will longer be trodden down, oppressed and misruled by beastly Gentile powers. The Kingdom of God and his Christ will then be established in the earth."[3]

Pastor Russell lived to see the year 1914 come and go—to witness the failure of his prediction. What was his reply to this? In 1916 he wrote: "The thought that the church would all be gathered to glory before October, 1914, certainly did have a very stimulating effect upon thousands, all of whom accordingly can praise the Lord—even for the mistake."[4]

Nevertheless, the date of 1914 has been retained. Jehovah's Witnesses claim that the overthrow of Gentile power began in that year, that Russell was wrong only in that he expected these things to happen more suddenly than they did. It is pointed out that it was in 1914 that World War I broke out.

The basis for the 1914 date was to be found, supposedly, in Leviticus 26. God told Israel that they would be blessed if they would obey him; but punished if they disobeyed. "And if you will not for all this harken unto me, but walk contrary unto me; then I...will chastise you SEVEN TIMES for your sins" (Lev. 26:28).

Russell taught these "seven times" meant seven symbolic or prophetic years of 360 days, that these "days" should be figured as years, and so seven times 360 years would be 2,520 years. Counting from 606 B.C.—when Israel went into Gentile captivity under Nebuchadnezzar—this would measure to 1914.

But the expression "seven times" does not appear once, but four times in Leviticus 26. If the expression means 2,520 years in one place, what about the others? If we multiply 2,520 years by four we would get 10,080 years that Israel would be punished!

The simple truth is that these references have nothing to do with periods of time, but with the severity of the punishment. If a child is spanked and the parent warns of punishment seven times as hard, this is a figure of speech expressing the severity of the punishment. So should the expression be

6

understood here. The same expression appears other places in the Old Testament and is never used to express a period of time.

Another problem with the 1914 date is this: the number 2,520, is based on 360 days to a year (lunar time)—7 times 360—yet in counting to 1914, years of *365* days (solar time) are used.

Take a close look into Leviticus. Take a look at the uses of the expression "seven times" in the other places it is used. Look at the Hebrew. Look at the awkward jumbling of seven times into years and these broken down into days and these multiplied by years to get the figure 2,520 years. Notice the inconsistency of using a year of 360 days to get the number 2,520, and then turning around and figuring a date based on years of 365 days by our calendar in order to arrive at 1914.

Some attempt to link the "seven times" of Leviticus 26 with the "seven times" mentioned in Nebuchadnezzar's dream (Dan. 4). But the expression here is from different Hebrew words. Nebuchadnezzar became insane and had his dwelling with the beasts of the field, after which he recovered and recognized that the Lord God was the supreme ruler. We see no reason to make these seven years mean 2,520 years, for what was prophesied was plainly fulfilled: "ALL this came upon the king Nebuchadnezzar....The same hour was the thing FULFILLED" (Dan. 4:28, 33).

If Leviticus or Daniel gave the year that Christ would return, why did Jesus say that he did not know the time of his return, but the Father only? If it was possible to determine the date from the Old Testament, we believe Jesus would have known it.

We do not doubt that there are many sincere and fine people within the Jehovah's Witness organization. It is too bad this movement, with its great zeal, has been plagued with numerous dates and theories based on them.

Returning to the east from Los Angeles, Pastor Russell died on a train at Pampa, Texas, in 1916—two years after the failure of the 1914 date. His successor, Joseph Franklin Rutherford, wrote a book *Millions Now Living Will Never Die*, published in 1920. In this book he taught that Abraham, Isaac,

7

and Jacob would be resurrected in 1925 to be made the visible and legal representatives of the new order of things on earth. An elaborate home, Beth-Sarim, the "House of the Princes," in San Diego, California, was to be occupied by these men. It was constructed with thick walls like a fortress. I have been to the mansion (a portion of which is seen in the accompanying photograph I took on June 24, 1977); Abraham, Isaac, and Jacob are not there!

Passing now from the Adventist and Jehovah's Witness dates, we will consider other dates that have been set over the centuries.

Tichonius, an early Christian writer, believed Christ would return in 381 A.D. In the book of Revelation, we read about "time, times, and the dividing of time." He figured a "time" as a century. Thus time, times, and the dividing of time would equal three and a half centuries. Then figuring—evidently—the time of Christ's ministry as the beginning for these 350 years, he arrived at the year 381 A. D.!

8

Hippolytus (170-236) and also Lactantius (250-330) believed the year 500 A.D. would be the time of the second coming of Christ. This was based on some erroneous dates given in the Septuagint translation of the Old Testament.

Many thought the year 1000 would either mark the coming of Christ or the appearance of Antichrist with the final judgment soon after. Figuring that the 1000 years of Revelation 20 referred to the Christian era, it was supposed that the year 1000 A.D.—1,000 years from the birth of Christ—would mark the end of that era. Some sold houses and lands, joined religious orders, and awaited the year 1000! Abbo of Fleury said that in his youth he had heard a preacher in Paris say that the Antichrist would appear in the year 1000 and that the end of the world would come shortly thereafter. "The rumor had filled almost the whole earth," he said. But the year 1000 came and went without the special events that some had predicted.

Of course there was some doubt regarding the calendar—it could be off about three or four years from the actual time that Christ was born. In view of this, some felt the year 1000 was only an approximate date. Consequently, in the year 1009 when the news of the conquest of Jerusalem by the Turks came, not a few supposed the end was near.

Some thought they should figure the Christian era as beginning with the *death* of Christ (rather than his birth), and this would place the end at approximately A.D. 1033. A terrible famine hit in this year and again some thought the end was upon them. In all these years between 1000 and 1033 there was considerable and unusual religious activity in connection with dates. Many felt relieved when this whole era had passed!

Using the number 1,260 in Revelation, in the middle ages, Joachim of Floris, an Italian monk, taught that the year 1260 would mark the purification of the church and the beginning of Christ's reign.

Michael Stiefel (1486-1567), a friend of Martin Luther, taught that Christ would come in judgment at 8 A.M. on October 19, 1533! Luther warned him against making such claims. Nevertheless, he continued and the news spread far and wide. Three days before, crowds began to assemble to await the final hours. Stiefel administered the Lord's supper. When the date failed, the disappointment knew no bounds. Some had neglected their work and lost their harvest.

He was bound with ropes and brought to Wittenberg, where some tried to sue him for damages. But Stiefel had given all his possessions away and had nowhere to go. Luther did not take it too seriously and received him into his house. A group of Anabaptists had also held the 1533 date, believing the millennium would begin that year.

During the first half of the Seventeenth Century, a number of Jews held the belief that the Messiah would appear in the year 1648. That year Sabbotai Zevi proclaimed himself as the promised Messiah, but the era of redemption that had been expected failed to materialize.

There were Christians scattered through various countries that expected the year 1666 to bring the end. Isaac Newton, noted for his research on gravity, set the date of 1715 for the second coming of Christ. William Whiston also held this view. When this failed, Whiston deferred the date to 1734. When this failed, he projected it to 1766—a date he did not live to see.

Johann Albrecht Bengel (1687-1752) believed that 666 was the length of years the beast system would rule. Since another scripture said it would be "forty-two months," he divided the one into the other, making each month equal 15 6/7 years of "prophetic time." Thus did he determine June 18, 1836 as the date of the overthrow of the Roman apostasy and the beginning of the millennium with Satan being bound. Apparently John Wesley favored this date also. Even though such calculations now appear inconsistent right on the surface, at that time there were a number of people who left their homes and moved to Southern Russia because of this date.

Joseph Wolff (1795-1862) traveled more widely than any other man of his time in announcing the soon coming of Christ—throughout Asia, Africa, Europe, and America, where he spoke before the assembled Congress. His message was that Christ "died for our sins, rose again, went to heaven, and shall come again, according to my opinion, in the year 1847!" Just before leaving America in 1837, someone asked him: "What will you say, Mr. Wolff, when 1847 arrives, if the millennium does not commence?" To this he replied, "Why, I shall say that Joseph Wolff was mistaken." And mistaken he was. He later abandoned the date of 1847.

The 1847 date had been taught in a book written by Johaan Philipp Petri in 1774. Like Miller's date, this was based on the 2300 days of Daniel 8. Philo Britannicus thought that the ultimate establishment of the kingdom of God would come in 1849. The Irvingites of England thought Christ would come in 1864.

It is interesting to notice the prophetic poem traditionally accredited to "Mother Shipton" of the Sixteenth Century, especially her date for the end of the world:

> Carriages without horses shall go,
>   and accidents fill the world with woe.
> Around the earth thoughts shall fly
>   in the twinkling of an eye;
> The world upside down shall be,
>   and gold be found at the root of a tree.
> Through hills man shall ride,
>   and no horse be at his side.
> Under water men shall walk,
>   shall ride, shall sleep, shall talk.
> In the air men shall be seen
>   in white, in black, in green;
> Iron in the water shall float,
>   as easily as a wooden boat.
> Gold shall be found and shown,
>   in a land that's not now known.
> Fire and water shall wonders do,
>   England shall at last admit a foe.
> The world to an end will come,
>   *in eighteen hundred and eighty-one.*

Actually, this edition of the poem was published in 1862 by Charles Hindley. It seemed that Mrs. Shipton, who had lived many years before, had predicted the automobile, telephone steam engine, the discovery of America, etc. But in 1873, Hindley confessed he had inserted additional lines! But whatever insight Mrs. Shipton may have had, again the folly of trying to date the end of the world is seen.

Joanna Southcott, who received much attention with her "visions," said Christ would come on October 19, 1884. A noted Boston pastor, Edward D. Griffin, spoke of "the complete establishment of the millennial kingdom" in about 1921 or 1922. This he publicly proclaimed in 1813, while the date was actually over a century away. This was different than most date setters who usually work dates to fit within a few years.

World War I ended on the *eleventh* hour of the *eleventh* day of the *eleventh* month (Nov.11, 1918). Not a few believed the world had entered her Eleventh Hour and the "Midnight" hour (Matt. 25:6) when Christ would come could not be far off.

Some supposed the date of 1962 could be obtained from the following passage: "From the time...the abomination that maketh desolate is set up, there shall be 1290 days. Blessed is he that waiteth, and cometh to the 1335 days" (Dan. 12:10-13). By figuring the days as years, taking the "abomination that maketh desolate" to be the building of the Muslim Dome of the Rock upon the old temple site in Jerusalem, 1,290 years could measure, roughly, to 1917, the year General Allenby ordered 100 planes to fly over Jerusalem and took the city without firing a shot. Then, because the prophecy said he would be "blessed" who would wait until the 1335 days, it was taught that the second coming of Christ would take place 45 years after 1917—that is, 1962.

When the date would have only been a few months away, I heard a man give 1964 as the year for the Lord's return. He had it all worked out on a large chart. Those who held the 1844 date were wrong, he said, only because they supposed that would be the end—that in reality it was only the "beginning" of the end. He pointed out that in the days of Noah there was a delay of 120 years before destruction came. So "as it was in the days of Noah"—adding 120 years to 1844—the end would be in 1964!

I once heard a preacher tell about a vision in which these words appeared before him like a neon sign: "It is later than you think!" At the time, he already believed the Lord would come within the next few years. Because of this vision, he was convinced the Lord was coming *very* soon. The problem is, this incident happened back in the 50s! How reliable are such visions?

I have before me a magazine which gives the account of a dream in which the earthly scene was changed from that of pollution and sin into a paradise: "I marveled at the radiantly glorious panorama before me. Suddenly, in final clarity, this date appeared before me: 1978!!!" The article then mentions that this date was in full agreement with the date set by William Branham.

Actually the date suggested by Branham was 1977: "I sincerely believe and maintain as a private student of the Word, along with Divine inspiration that 1977 ought to terminate the world system and usher in the millennium."[5]

Years ago a preacher on the radio said we may not know the "day," but this does not mean we can't know the NIGHT! He claimed Christ would come on the night of the Day of Atonement. In order to be ready, he taught that a person must be awake and watching—physically and literally—on this night!

Dates that are set for around the year 2,000 are based on the 6,000 year theory. Because the scriptures speak of six days of work and the seventh as the sabbath, figuring a day is with the Lord as a thousand years, some believe 6,000 years of human history will mark the end of the age, to be followed by a thousand years of rest. This is no new teaching. It can be found in the ancient book called *Secrets of Enoch* (chapter 32). Later it was referred to in the *Epistle of Barnabas*.

The Bible says that "one day is with the Lord as a thousand years," but it *also* says, "and a thousand years as one day" (2 Peter 3:8). This could not prove that a day equals a thousand years, any more than it could prove that a thousand years equals a day. It simply shows that God is not limited by our ideas of time.

It is generally figured that Christ was born approximately 4,000 years from the creation of Adam and that the year 2,000 will mark the close of 6,000 years. But according to the Jewish reckoning, mentioned in the *Encyclopedia Britannica* (article, "Chronology"), creation was the year 3761 B.C. If correct, the year 6,000 would still be almost three centuries away!

If we figure a generation as forty years (cf. Heb. 3:9, 10), in 6,000 years this would only be 150 generations. While, admittedly, it may be intended as a figure of speech, the Bible uses the term "a thousand generations" (Deut. 7:9; 1 Chron. 16:15). At 40 years to a generation, this would be 40,000 years!

When I was about 13 years old I remember hearing the teaching that some major event happens every 2,000 years. Two thousand years after the creation of Adam, there was the flood. Two thousand years after this, Christ was born. Two thousand years more would undoubtedly be the second coming of Christ. But this breaks down if we simply add up the ages the Bible gives in Genesis: from the creation of Adam to the flood was 1,656 years—not 2,000 years.

Some believe the Jews are "God's clock"—that somehow God's schedule is all tied in with Jewish happenings. Prior to 1948, they taught that the prophetic clock had quit running because the Jews were out of their land. As soon as the Jews would be back in their land, with their own nation, the rapture of the church would take place. Well, this viewpoint experienced embarrassment in 1948 when the nation of Israel was established.

Then some said the church was not taken out because only a part of *Jerusalem* was in "Jewish hands." This also faced embarrassment in 1967 when the Jews took the whole city in the famous six day war.

Since the first edition of *His Truth is Marching On* was published—in 1977—still more dates have been set and *continue* to be set for the return of Christ. Noteable among these have been the widely-distributed books *88 Reasons Why the Rapture Will Be in 1988* (Edgar Whisenant) and *1994?* (Harold Camping).

It should be apparent that the methods of interpretation whereby such dates are set are faulty. Some become so intrigued with these things, they lose all balance. If a date doesn't fit one way, they stretch it out another. I appeal to all Christians—especially young Christians and new converts—not to become too alarmed or upset by such calculations.

Paul said: "Despise not prophesyings," but the next verse says: "Prove all things" (1 Thess. 5:20, 21). Surely the two statements go together. When dates are promoted in a dogmatic way, the results have often been unfortunate. Who

14

hasn't read newspaper stories of groups which set a date and then lock themselves up in a house or escape to some remote area awaiting the end? Sometimes the police have to finally intervene as children are not sent to school or bills are not paid! There have been suicides because of failed dates.

History teaches some important lessons if we will only learn them.

In spite of the fact that many dates have been set—and have failed—we share with all Christians the grand and glorious hope of his coming! We are content, however, to leave the "times and seasons" in his hands, believing that some things God *reveals,* and some things he *conceals.* We will seek to "occupy until he comes" and not live in fear about trying to escape to Petra, or Israel, or some desert place. We do not pretend to know the day nor hour—or year!—of his coming. We do believe, though, that with every breath we draw that his coming is getting closer all the time. As Paul said: "Now is our salvation *nearer* than when we believed" (Rom. 13:11).

Chapter 2

"SEVEN WOMEN SHALL TAKE HOLD OF ONE MAN"—Future or Fulfilled?

"And in that day seven women shall take hold of one man, saying, We will eat our own bread, and wear our own apparel: only let us be called by thy name, to take away our reproach" (Isa. 4:1).

When Isaiah said seven women "shall" take hold of one man, this was, *at that time,* a prophecy for the future. But is it *still* future? Our answer (which we believe is clearly indicated in the scriptures) is that this prophecy was fulfilled back in Old Testament times.

The women mentioned were "daughters of Zion." The setting for the prophecy was Jerusalem and Judah (Isa. 3:1). This being the case, the prophecy does not pertain to London, Hong Kong, Moscow, New York, Los Angeles, or Salt Lake City. Nor was Isaiah 4:1 a rebuke for polygamy. There were many men during the period of the Old Testament who had more than one wife—among them such noted men as Gideon, David, Solomon, Jacob, and Abraham.

The reason why seven women would take hold of one man was because there would be a *shortage of men*—a shortage due to *war.* In the immediate context it is written: "Thy MEN shall fall by the sword, and thy mighty in the WAR"—war linked with Jerusalem and Judah (Isa. 3:25).

Because Isaiah 4:1 is actually a continuation of the thought expressed in Chapter 3, it could have rightly been included as the last verse of that chapter. Adam Clarke has pointed out: "The division of the chapter has interrupted the prophet's discourse, and broken it off almost in the midst of the sentence." Ferrar Fenton's translation includes Isaiah 4:1 as part of Chapter 3. Failing to follow the line of thought through from

16

Chapter 3 (because of the chapter division), some have thought of Isaiah 4:1 as a kingdom blessing. But such a shortage of men would hardly be a blessing!

Others have applied the scripture about seven women taking hold of one man to the seven churches of Revelation who take hold of one man, Christ. Being called by his name (Christians) to take away their reproach; some wear their own apparel (self righteousness) and eat their own bread (following their own ideas instead of his doctrines). Victorinus, an early church father, said: "The seven women are seven churches, receiving his bread, and clothed with his apparel." He spoke of the bread as the Holy Spirit; the garments as immortality. But whatever merit these ideas may have, we need look no further than Old Testament times for the actual fulfillment.

Isaiah's prophetic ministry spanned the reigns of several kings in Judah: Uzziah, Jotham, Ahaz, and Hezekiah (Isa. 1:1). Since the death of Uzziah is recorded in Chapter 6—"In the year that king Uzziah died I saw also the Lord..."—it would appear that the prophecy under consideration was toward the early part of Isaiah's ministry, some time before king Uzziah died.

Within a few years, Ahaz came to the throne and led the nation away from God. Judgment came upon the nation of Judah. Many of their men were killed in war. Ahaz "was delivered...into the hand of the king of Syria...and into the hand of the king of Israel, who smote him with a great SLAUGHTER. For Pekah the son of Remallah slew in Judah an HUNDRED AND TWENTY THOUSAND in one day, which were all valiant MEN..." (2 Chron. 28:1-8).

The passage continues, using an elaborate figure of speech to show the immensity of the slaughter: "You have SLAIN them in a rage that reached up unto heaven"! There was a shortage of men in Judah because of WAR.

By the time Hezekiah's son, Manasseh, reigned, the shortage of men was so great in Jerusalem and Judah that we read: "Their WIDOWS are increased to me ABOVE THE SAND OF THE SEAS"! (Jer. 15:8). In other words, there were vast multitudes of women—daughters of Zion—who no longer had husbands.

Thus we see that in the years that followed Isaiah's prophecy (chapter 3 through 4:1), the nation of Judah suffered the loss of many, many men. With this situation, we can understand why an expression about seven women taking hold of one man was given.

In those days it was considered a great reproach for a woman to go through life without marriage and children (Gen. 30:23; 1 Sam. 1; Lk. 1:25). The women in Isaiah 4:1 were willing to share a husband, were willing to make their own living, eat their own bread, wear their own apparel—as long as they could be married and take away their "reproach."

I do not think we need to understand that exactly "seven" women took hold of one man in each case. Rather this numerical ratio is an expression to show the shortage of men in proportion to women. We might compare Zechariah 8:23 in which it was said that "ten" men would take hold of a man who is called a Jew. In neither case is mathematical exactness required. The point is the CONTRAST these expressions convey.

The third chapter of Isaiah (which leads up to the statement in Isaiah 4:1), predicted hard times that would come upon Jerusalem and Judah. The historical account is given in the book of Lamentations—often using wording very similar to the prophecy.

BIBLICAL FULFILLMENTS

The prophecy in Isaiah said: "And her gates shall lament and mourn; and she being desolate shall sit upon the ground" (Isa. 3:26). The fulfillment: "All her gates are desolate...he hath made me desolate...mourning and lamentation...the elders of the daughter of Zion sit upon the ground" (Lam. 1:4, 13; 2:5, 10).

Isaiah said their ornaments and fine clothing would be taken away; the "beauty" of the "daughters of Zion" would depart (Isa. 3:16, 24). The fulfillment: "From the daughter of Zion all her beauty is departed....Jerusalem remembered...all her pleasant things that she had in the days of old....They that did feed delicately are desolate in the streets: they that were brought up in scarlet embrace dunghills" (Lam. 1:6, 7; 4:5).

In the stress of the times, Isaiah said their bread would be scarce (Isa. 3:1-7). In Lamentations we read: "All her people sigh, they seek bread; they have given their pleasant things for meat" (Lam. 1:11).

Instead of fine clothing, Isaiah said they would have a "girding of sackcloth" (Isa. 3:24). This was fulfilled, for it is recorded: "...they have girded themselves with sackcloth" (Lam. 2:10).

Isaiah said: "Behold, the Lord...doth take away from Jerusalem...the mighty man, and the man of war," etc. (Isa. 3:1, 2). In Lamentations, we read: "The Lord hath trodden under foot all my mighty men in the midst" (Lam. 1:15). And the shortage of men that resulted is seen in the following cry: "We are orphans and fatherless, our mothers are as widows ....Our fathers have sinned, and are not" (Lam. 5:3, 7). "The punishment of thine iniquity IS accomplished, 0 daughter of Zion" (Lam. 4:22). In view of such statements, can there be any doubt as to the fulfillment of the prophecy under consideration?

ANCIENT CLOTHING STYLES

Another reason the prophecy should be understood within an historical context is seen in the description of the women's clothing. It is definitely not a description of modern dress!

"The Lord will take away the bravery of their tinkling ornaments about their feet, and their cauls [a netting for the hair], and their round tires like the moon..." These tires were round pendants suspended from the neck, probably made of gold. In Judges 8:21, the same word is translated "ornaments" —gold ornaments shaped like the moon in honor of the moon-faced goddess Astarte—in this case, suspended from the necks of camels.

The list continues: "The chains [pendants for the ears, especially of pearls], and the bracelets, and the mufflers [long veils], the bonnets, and the ornaments of the legs [ankle-chains], and the headbands, and the tablets [perfume boxes], and the earrings, the rings, and nose jewels [rings set with jewels hanging from a hole in the left nostril], the changeable suits of apparel [festival robes], and the mantles [cloaks], and the wimples [shawls], and the crisping pins..."

Crisping pins? Some have associated "crisping pins" with the idea of curling, or perhaps the use of a crimping iron. Some

19

have used this as a text against women using hair curlers. But none of these things can be based on the Hebrew text. Strong's Concordance says that the word carries the meaning of *cut out*, or *hollow*, and thus implies a *pocket.* It is translated "satchels" by Goodspeed and "purses" by Moffatt. The same word in 2 Kings 5:23 is translated "bags."

The list continues: "...the glasses [mirrors], and the fine linen, and the hoods, and the veils" (Isa. 3:18-23).

The style of dress here described does not refer to our times, but to the way women of means dressed in the time of Isaiah. Since this fine clothing would be taken away in the stress which was to come upon Jerusalem and Judah, the fulfillment of this prophecy is definitely an Old Testament fulfillment.

THE AUTOMOBILE AND MODERN INVENTIONS?

During World War II, when there was a shortage of rubber for automobile tires, some could not pass up the temptation to quote a few words from this passage in Isaiah! "The Lord will take away...their round tires like the moon" (Isa. 3:18). Even though the setting for this chapter was an Old Testament war in which Jerusalem and Judah were involved, and even though the "round tires" were mentioned within a list of ornaments worn by women in Isaiah's time, the vague similarity in wording caused some to believe prophecy was being fulfilled before their eyes! I don't suppose any real harm is done by such ideas, but we can only say this is obviously not the correct way to understand the scriptures.

Isaiah's mention of "round tires" can no more refer to automobile tires, than his mention of "mufflers" can mean a part of the exhaust system of an automobile, or "hoods" to that portion that covers the motor!

I can remember hearing as a young boy that the automobile was mentioned in the Bible. The passage that is still sometimes quoted for this is Nahum 2:4: "The chariots shall rage in the streets, they shall jostle one against another in the broadways: they shall seem like torches, they shall run like the lightnings." Some suppose the prophet used the term "chariots" because this term was familiar to him, but what he really saw was the automobile, rapid travel, and wrecks on modern-day freeways!

The very first verse of Nahum, however, indicates that this was NOT a prophecy about our time, but was about the ancient city of NINEVEH. Though much of the prophecy is given in the poetic imagery which was more common to that time, it is plainly a prophecy pronouncing the overthrow and destruction of the ancient city of Nineveh. *This happened in 612 B.C.!*

The accompanying drawing of an Assyrian war chariot illustrates what Nahum spoke of —chariots pulled by horses, driven by horse-men with whips, who also had swords and spears (Nah. 3:2, 3). In the stress of the conflict, these war chariots would move quickly—  symbolically likened to lightning—and would jostle against each other in the broadways of Nineveh. Expressions such as: "The chariots shall rage in the streets" (Nah. 2:4) were commonly applied to chariots in ancient battles, as, for example, "Come up, horses; and *rage,* chariots; and let the mighty men come forth..." (Jer. 46:9). When Nineveh was destroyed, it was burned with fire, as were also the chariots (Nah. 3:15, 2:13)! This was not a prediction about automobiles.

A book written in 1917, used the same passage in Nahum as though it were a train pulled with a steam locomotive. "The shield is made red" was said to be the headlight of the train. "The valiant men in scarlet" were the engineer and fireman —both of them appearing in scarlet or red from the flames of the firebox when the door was opened to put in more coal! "He shall recount his worthies" was the conductor collecting tickets. "They shall stumble in their walk" were people stumbling as they walked through the moving train. The reference to the "palace" was wrested from its obvious meaning and applied to the Pullman "palace" cars, as they were sometimes called![6]

More recently, some have sought to find the airplane in the Bible. Isaiah 58:14 has been quoted: "I will cause you to ride upon the high places of the earth." But this is simply a figure of

21

speech. The same was said of Israel after coming out of Egypt: "He made him ride on the high places of the earth" (Deut. 32:13; Ex. 19:4). Unless we are ready to teach that Moses and the children of Israel had airplanes in which to fly, we should not stretch this figure of speech beyond its intended meaning.

Others suppose the Bible predicted the following:

DEEP SEA DIVERS—"hast thou walked in the search of the depth?" (Job 38:16).

ELECTRICITY—"who hath divided...a way for the lightning of thunder?" (verse 25).

TELEPHONE, TELEVISION, RADIO—"Canst thou send lightnings, that they may go, and say unto thee, Here we are?" (verses 34, 35).

SUBMARINE—"...and makes men as the fish of the sea, as the creeping things, that have no ruler over them" (Hab. 1:14).

DRAWBRIDGES, RIVER LOCKS—"the gates of the rivers shall be opened" (Nah. 2:6).

FLYING SAUCERS, UFOs—"...brightness...a wheel in the middle of a wheel...lifted up from the earth" (Ezek. 1).

Though these verses present some interesting similarities, considered in context, it is doubtful whether any of them refer to modern inventions. What is more important, more wonderful, more thrilling, more far-reaching than whether the Bible mentions—or does not mention such things—is that grand truth expressed in the best-known verse in the Bible: "For God so loved the world, that he gave his only begotten Son, that whosoever believeth in him should not perish, but have EVERLASTING LIFE" (John 3:16).

Chapter 3

THE BATTLE OF EZEKIEL 38 AND 39
—Future or Fulfilled?

"THUS SAITH THE Lord God; behold, I am against thee, O Gog, the chief prince of Meshech and Tubal: and I will turn you back...and all thy army...Persia, Ethiopia, and Libya with them...Gomer, and all his bands; the house of Togarmah of the north quarters...in the latter years thou shalt come...against the mountains of Israel...Sheba, and Dedan, and the merchants of Tarshish...shall say unto thee, Art thou come to take a spoil...to take away cattle and goods?" (Ezek. 38, 39).

Some of my best friends believe this prophecy conclusively teaches that Russia is going to come down and invade the nation of Israel—possibly in the near future! Some prophecy teachers have put such emphasis on this view, they have led people to assume it is a clear, undisputed, fundamental teaching of the Bible! The idea that the Bible teaches that Russia will soon invade Israel may even influence the political thinking of some people.

This view has been taught on radio and television programs; it appears in the notes of certain reference Bibles dedicated to the futurist viewpoint; it has been taught in Sunday night prophetic specials and illustrated on elaborate charts!

One group on January 2, 1968, sent a letter to Premier Aleksei Kosygin by registered airmail and also printed copies by the thousands for distribution in booklet form. "This is a warning!" the letter says, "The God of the universe is nearly finished with taking your abuse. You and your comrades are destined *soon* to lead your nation into total disaster as reward for the evil you have perpetuated." The writer probably really believed it would be "soon" that Russians would attack Israel where they would meet "total disaster." Well, that was in 1968,

23

a lot of changes have come, but nothing to fit the things this booklet threatened.

It is not our intent to make light of fellow Christians who sincerely hold such views. However, certain questions are apparent: Does Ezekiel 38 teach that Russia will invade the State of Israel in the near future? Or does this chapter describe an *ancient* battle?

I will state my position quite clearly: I do not believe Ezekiel 38 has anything to do with Russia invading the modern State of Israel. Instead, there is internal evidence that the setting for this prophecy must be back during the OLD TESTAMENT era. Its description fits that of an ANCIENT battle.

Because the prophecy uses terms like "latter years" and "latter days" (Ezek. 38:8, 16), some immediately rule out any historical fulfillment. But the word that is translated "latter," while designating something "future" (Strong's Concordance, #319), does not in itself define WHEN in the future. The Moffatt translation says: "...after many a day, and after many a year," while Lamsa gives the passage as: "the later years." Simply put, what Ezekiel prophesied would occur *later on*—from the time he wrote.

Moses told Israel: "I know that after my death you will utterly corrupt yourselves, and turn aside from the way which I have commanded you; and evil will befall you in *the latter days;* because you will do evil in the sight of the Lord, to provoke him to anger through the work of your hands" (Deut. 31:29). Those "latter days" came some years later, following the death of Joshua, as we read in Judges 2:19, 20: "And it came to pass...they corrupted themselves...in following other gods to serve them...and the anger of the Lord was hot against Israel."

Daniel interpreted Nebuchadnezzar's dream of an image symbolizing what would happen in the "latter days," or, as the next verse says, "what should come to pass hereafter" (Dan. 2:28, 29). Since the image represented four successive world empires—all of which came into existence before the first coming of Christ—the expression "latter days" clearly meant "later" from their viewpoint—not something that is still future from our point in time.

Many judgments were pronounced upon Israel in Jeremiah 30, all of which happened—according to other scriptures. This chapter then closes with the words: "...in the latter days you shall consider it" (verse 24). The latter days in this instance, were clearly those days following these judgments, the captivity, and deliverance from captivity.

Deliverance for Moab and Elam was also promised in the "latter days" (Jer. 48:47; 49:39), which, in context, could have only happened in what we now call history.

The Temple which the Israelites built upon their return from the Babylonian captivity was called the "latter house" as compared to the "former" house before the captivity (Hag. 1:9). The prophets that had warned them before the captivity were referred to as "the former prophets" (Zech. 1:4; 7:7, 12). Those days before the captivity are spoken of as "the former days" (Zech. 8:11) which would mark the days after the captivity—in comparison—as the later or latter days.

In view of these things, I think it is evident that the expression "latter days" used in Ezekiel's prophecy, does not require a fulfillment in modern times.

Because the Israelites in Ezekiel 38 are described as being "brought forth out of the *nations*" (Ezek. 38:8), some suppose this requires a modern-day fulfillment. The argument goes like this: At one time the Israelites were brought out of Egypt, later they were brought out of Babylon, but here they are brought forth out of the nations (plural). It was after 70 A.D. that they were scattered to the nations, and did not become a nation again until 1948, so this is when they were gathered out of the nations.

This is faulty reasoning, for at the time of the Babylonian captivity they were also scattered to many nations—not just Babylon. We can see this right within other chapters of Ezekiel. Their cities would be destroyed and they would be scattered *among the nations* whither they shall be carried captives" (Ezek. 6:6-9). They would be removed and "go into captivity ...among the nations," and their leader would be taken to Babylon (Ezek. 12:10-15).

But, there was also the promise of being again gathered from the nations—not in 1948 A.D.—but following the seventy year captivity! "For thus saith the Lord, that after seventy years be accomplished at Babylon I will visit you...and I will turn away your captivity, and I will gather you from ALL THE NATIONS...and I will bring you again into the place whence I caused you to be carried away captive" (Jer. 29:10-14). In view of such statements, the reference about a people "brought forth out of the nations" does not require a fulfillment in modern times.

What, then, are our reasons for believing that the setting for the battle described by Ezekiel was after their return from the seventy years captivity? Why do we believe this battle pertained to Old Testament times and not to a future fulfillment? The reasons are as follows:

FIRST, the invading soldiers who make up the armies of this passage would be riding on HORSES! "And thou shalt come from thy place out of the north parts, thou, and many people with thee, ALL OF THEM RIDING UPON HORSES, a great company, and a mighty army" (Ezek. 38:15).

We know that the house of Togormah (which is included in the invasion) was in possession of horses and traded them at Tyre (Ezek. 27:14). Horses were commonly used in ancient battles (as in the accompanying illustration), numerous references to such being mentioned in the Bible and history. Even up until comparatively recent times, different nations maintained some small cavalry units—but no longer. The *World Book Encyclopedia* (article: "cavalry") says: "The expense of maintaining horses and the greater speed and mobility of motorized units made horse cavalry obsolete by the mid-1900's."

To those who think Ezekiel 38 is a prophecy for the near future, I ask: Will major armies of the world revert back to using horses in battle?

We should carefully notice also that this prophecy not only mentions soldiers on horses—as though perhaps a few soldiers might be on horses—but it says, "ALL of them riding upon horses"! It does not say part of them would be on horses, or a few of them, or even many of them; it says ALL of them upon horses! They are not flying in airplanes or helicopters. They are not traveling in jeeps. They are not in tanks. They are not in ships or submarines. These troops are not moving in buses or trains. All of them are riding on horses!

26

SECOND, the time of this invasion is described as a time when Israel would be dwelling in peace. The enemy forces are pictured as saying: "I will go up to the land of unwalled villages; I will go to them that are at REST, that dwell SAFELY, all of them dwelling without walls, and having neither bars nor gates" (Ezek. 38:11).

There were times within the Old Testament when Israel enjoyed times of rest and safety. But the modern nation of Israel is one of the most troubled spots on earth! Repeatedly it is in the news as a place of war, trouble, and insecurity. The picture has been anything but one of rest and safety. If these conditions were to change, such changes would have to stand the test of time, over a period of years, before anyone would be saying of the State of Israel: "I will go to them that are at rest, that dwell safely"!

Notice also that the enemy is pictured as saying he would go to the land of "unwalled villages." In times of peace, apparently, the villages within the land of Israel did not have walls. In the days of Esther we read about "the Jews of the villages, that dwelt in the unwalled towns" (Esth. 9:19).

Though cities commonly had walls, it was not uncommon for *villages* to be without walls (Lev. 25:29, 31; Deut. 3:5). During a time of peace, and with villages without walls, we can see how the enemy could refer to this as the land of unwalled villages. But notice the implication! The time of this prophecy would be when *some* lands and countries *did* have villages with protective walls. It is a comparative statement!

In our day, neither cities nor villages depend on walls for protection. Walls, so commonly known and used in ancient times—such as those around Jerusalem, Jericho, Babylon, or Nineveh—would now be obsolete. Would an enemy in our time speak of going up to a land of unwalled villages—a relative term? No, for all lands are now this way.

THIRD, notice the purpose of this invasion against Israel. The enemy was to obtain, among other things, CATTLE! "And thou shalt say...I will go up to the land...to take a spoil, and to take a prey; to turn thine hand upon the desolate places that are now inhabited...to carry away silver and gold, to take away CATTLE and goods, to take a great spoil" (Ezek. 38:11-13).

Dramatic sermons have sometimes portrayed the Russians as coming against Israel to get wealth from minerals in the Dead Sea. Or the word "spoil" is turned into "oil"! But Israel is not an oil producing country. The invading forces here, come riding on horses and stealing cattle (among other things). This fits the *ancient* reasons for invading another land, but can hardly apply to our day. Does anyone really believe this prophecy is talking about a bunch of Russian cattle rustlers?

FOURTH, the weapons used by this army are PRIMITIVE weapons. All of the soldiers ride on horses, "ALL of them clothed with all sorts of armor, even a great company with bucklers and shields, ALL of them handling swords...ALL of them with shield and helmet" (Ezek. 38:4, 5), using bows and arrows and spears (Ezek. 39:9).

These soldiers fight with bows and arrows. They handle swords. They wear armor. They have shields to protect them against arrows shot from bows. Such a detailed description can hardly fit modern warfare. The accompanying illustrations show the type of weapons that were used at the period under consideration.

FIFTH, these primitive weapons—bows, arrows, shields, and spears—were made out of materials which could be used as *firewood* (Ezek. 39:9, 10)! Modern weapons are not make of wood.

In an effort to uphold the futurist view-point, some strange explanations have been presented to justify the idea of weapons made of wood. It is pointed out that a wood product called lignostone, put together under great pressure, is very strong and durable. There is also a wood called Lignum Vitae obtained from a tree which grows in Latin America. Because its grain interlocks, it is almost impossible to split. It has been used for shaft bearings in steam ships, mallets, and furniture casters.

And of course there is Howard Hughes' giant Hercules Flying Boat, nicknamed the "Spruce Goose," which was built of wood. The plane was flown by Hughes on November 2, 1947, skimming along 70 feet above the water for less than a mile —then placed in storage for years. Later, when it was on display in Long Beach, California, I saw this monstrous curiosity.

So, the theory is that the Russians might make weapons from some treated form of very strong wood. But would they make bows, arrows, and spears out of such? What match could these be against modern weapons? If the reader is satisfied that this was what Ezekiel meant, this is his right. I can only say that I find these explanations far from satisfactory.

SIXTH, the time of this battle was when people used WOOD for fuel. "And they that dwell in the cities of Israel shall go forth, and shall set on fire and burn the weapons, both the shields and the bucklers, the bows and the arrows, and the handstaves, and the spears, and they shall burn them with fire seven years: so that they shall take no wood out of the field, neither cut down any out of the forests; for they shall burn the weapons with fire" (Ezek. 39:9, 10).

This is not a picture of modern times. How many people depend on wood for heating and cooking? Today, coal, gas, or electricity are generally used. The trend in the future will not be a return to cutting down trees for fuel—they are too valuable for building and other purposes. Besides, a return to burning wood for heating would only add to air pollution. In the future, new sources of energy will be developed. Already solar heating is widely used in the State of Israel.

But the picture we are given in Ezekiel 38 and 39 is of ancient times—when men went into the field and forest *looking for wood to burn.* This does not fit modern times.

In the prophecy, we read of "GOG, the chief prince of Meshech and Tubal" (Ezek. 39:1). The meaning of the word "Gog" is unknown. The root from which the term is derived is unknown. Possibly it is a veiled name or title, like emperor or king.

Concerning the various tribes which would make up the army under "Gog," however, we do have information. Magog, Gomer, Tubal, Meshech, Togarmah, Tarshish, Javan, Sheba, and Dedan were all grandsons or great grandsons of Noah. This is explained in Genesis 10:1-7. Just as the descendants of Jacob (Israel) were called the children of Israel, or later, simply Israel, so these various names were passed on down and named upon different tribes that descended from Noah.

By today's standards, none of these people were very far from the land of Israel. We know they were close enough to carry on commerce among themselves. Ezekiel 27 tells of the products they traded at the city of Tyre, specifically mentioning Persia, Tarshish, Tubal, Meshech, Togarmah, Dedan, and Sheba. The accompanying map shows where these various tribes were located.

Those who hold the futurist view concerning Ezekiel 38, attempt to locate these tribes in distant lands to which they

30

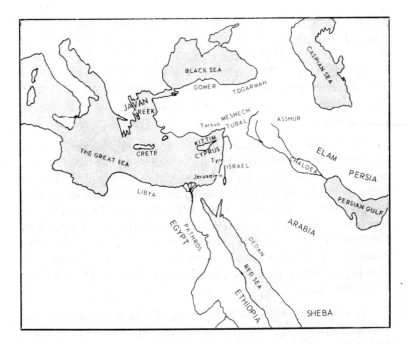

may have migrated over many centuries since the days of Ezekiel. This procedure is often based on a very sketchy or imagined line of evidence. And, even though several *different* tribes are mentioned, the strongest efforts are made to link the prophecy with RUSSIA!

The basic argument for this is based on the word translated "chief" in Ezekiel 38:3: "Behold, I am against thee, O Gog, the *chief* prince of Meshech and Tubal." The word chief is, in Hebrew, *ro'sh*. In the Revised Version it was left in the Hebrew form as though it was the name of a place; that is, Gog was called the "prince of Rosh, Meshech and Tubal." And so, some have supposed that Rosh is simply another way of saying Russia! But *ro'sh*, meaning "head," is a very common word and appears in the Old Testament OVER SIX HUNDRED TIMES! It seems very doubtful that it could mean Russia in this one instance.

Once it is assumed that Gog is the head or leader of Russia, then we are told that Meshech means Moscow! Again, this is doubtful. "Moscow" comes from the Moscovites and is a Finnish name. Moscow was first mentioned in ancient documents in

1147 A. D. when a small village. Some think Tubal means Tobolsk, but this is only a similarity in sound. Tobolsk was founded in 1587 A. D. Some think Gomer means Germany. It is true the words "Gomer" and "Germany" both begin with a "G." So does guesswork. The words Heaven and Hell both begin with the letter "H," but this does not make them the same place!

Neither can the mention that this invasion would come from the *north* prove that Russia is meant. Of course Russia is north of Israel. But many times cities within Israel were attacked from the north, the word north commonly appearing in this connection (Jer. 6:22, etc.). The house of Togarmah was located in "the north quarters" (Ezek. 38:6) and the attack by Gog would "come up from the north parts" (Ezek. 39:2). But some of the invading tribes were located *south* of Israel. Yet this point is often by-passed by those who place all the emphasis on Russia.

It may very well be that descendants of some of these tribes migrated north into what is now Russia. Some of these tribes may still be represented by certain people, while others are no longer a distinct people. There is much uncertainty and lack of real proof for many of these things. But where these people may have migrated is beside the point. If the proper setting for the battle of Ezekiel pertains to Old Testament times, it is clear that modern-day Russia has no place in the prophecy.

Some will recall that Gog and Magog are also mentioned in Revelation 20:8, 9. The *imagery* in Revelation is doubtless based on Ezekiel 38 and 39, but there is no reason to believe both refer to the same battle, for the following reasons:

1. In Ezekiel, Gog is a prince. In Revelation, Gog is a nation.

2. In Ezekiel, Gog is spoken of as coming against Israel with people from various countries around Israel; in Revelation, Gog and Magog are pictured as nations in the four quarters of the earth, in number as the sands of the sea.

3. In Ezekiel, Gog and his troops come against Israel, a people who have returned from captivity and are dwelling without walls; in Revelation, Gog and Magog go up on the breadth of the earth and compass the city of the saints.

4. In Ezekiel the enemy is Gog *of* the land of Magog; in Revelation, Gog *and* Magog.

5. In Ezekiel, Gog's troops are defeated in Israel and the people burn the remaining weapons for seven years; in Revelation, Gog and Magog are destroyed by fire from God out of heaven. In this case, it seems, wooden weapons would be destroyed then and there, not leaving a supply of firewood for the next seven years.

It is not uncommon for the imagery of Revelation to be based on Old Testament subjects or places. The "Jezebel" of Revelation is not the same woman as in Kings. The "Sodom" in Revelation is not the same Sodom as in Genesis. The "Babylon" in Revelation is not the Babylon of Daniel. The "New Jerusalem" in Revelation cannot mean the old Jerusalem. But in each instance, the former serves as a type. The woman Jezebel had already died, the cities of Sodom and Babylon had already been overthrown, and (in our opinion) the battle of Ezekiel 38 and 39 (if a literal battle) had already met its fulfillment within an Old Testament setting.

But what about fulfillment? Do we know for certain that the very people mentioned did indeed attack Israel within the Old Testament era and met with the fate described? Can such be confirmed by secular history?

I will give here the notes suggested by Adam Clarke, a noted theologian whose commentary on the Bible has been in circulation well over a century. He believed that Gog symbolized Antiochus Epiphanes, whose armies were overthrown by Israelite forces about 400 years after Ezekiel prophesied.[7]

Ezekiel 38, verse 3: "Behold, I am against thee, 0 Gog, the chief prince of Meshech and Tubal." These probably mean the auxiliary forces, over which Antiochus was supreme.

Verse 4: "I will turn you back...and all your army." Thy enterprise will fail.

Verse 5: "Persia, Ethiopia, and Libya with them..." That a part of Persia was tributary to Antiochus, see 1 Macc. 3:31. That Ethiopia, and Libya were auxiliaries of Antiochus is evident from Daniel 11:43: "The Libyans and Ethiopians shall be at his steps."

Verse 6: "Gomer and all his bands; the house of Togarmah..." The Cimmerians and Turcomanians and other northern nations.

Verse 8: "In the latter years thou shalt come into the land of ...Israel." This was fulfilled about 400 years later.

Verse 9: "Thou shalt ascend and come like a storm." It is observable that Antiochus is thus spoken of by Daniel, chapter 11:40: The king of the north (Antiochus) shall come against the king of the south (the king of Egypt) like a whirlwind.

Verse 10: "It shall also come to pass that at the same time shall things come into thy mind, and thou shalt think an evil thought." Antiochus purposed to invade and destroy Egypt, as well as Judea; see Daniel 11:31, 32, 36.

Verse 12: "To take a spoil..." When Antiochus took Jerusalem he gave the pillage of it to his soldiers, and spoiled the temple of its riches, which were immense. Josephus, *Wars* (Book I, chapter 1).

Verse 13: "Sheba, and Dedan." The Arabians, anciently great plunderers; and "Tarshish," the inhabitants of the famous isle Tartessus, the most noted merchants of the time. They are here represented as coming to Antiochus before he undertook the expedition, and bargaining for the spoils of the Jews. "Art thou come to take a spoil, to carry away silver and gold, cattle, and goods?"

Verse 16: "When I shall be sanctified in thee, 0 Gog." By the defeat of his troops under Lysias, his general. 1 Macc. 3:32, 33, etc. and chapter 8:6.

Verse 21: "And I will call for a sword against him." Meaning Judas Maccabeus, who defeated his army under Lysias, making a horrible carnage.

Verse 22: "Great hailstones, fire, and brimstone." These are probably figurative expressions, to signify that the whole tide of the war should be against him, and that his defeat and slaughter should be great.

Ezekiel 39, verse 2: "...and leave but the sixth part of thee." The margin has, strike thee with six plagues; or, draw thee back with a hook of six teeth.

Verse 3: "I will smite thy bow out of thy left hand, and will cause thine arrows to fall out of thy right hand." The Persians whom Antiochus had in his army, chapter 38:5, were famous as archers, and they may be intended here. The bow is held in the left hand; the arrow is pulled and discharged by the right.

Verse 6: "I will send a fire on Magog," on Syria, I will destroy the Syrian troops. "And among them that dwell carelessly in the isles," the auxiliary troops that came to Antiochus from the borders of the Euxine Sea.

Verse 7: "And I will not let them pollute my holy name any more." See on 1 Macc. 1:11, etc., how Antiochus had profaned the temple, insulted Jehovah and his worship. God permitted that as a scourge to his disobedient people; but now the scourger shall be scourged, and he shall pollute the sanctuary no more.

"They shall burn them [the weapons] with fire seven years." These may be figurative expressions, after the manner of the Asiatics, whose language abounds with such descriptions. They occur everywhere in the prophets. As to the number seven, it is only a certain for an indeterminate number. But as the slaughter was great, and the bows, arrows, quivers, shields, bucklers, handstaves, and spears were in vast multitudes, it must have taken a long time to gather them up in the different parts of the fields of battle, and the roads in which the Syrians had retreated throwing away their arms as they proceeded; so there might have been a long time employed in collecting and burning them. And as all seem to have been doomed to the fire, there might have been some found at different intervals during the seven years mentioned.

Verse 11: "The valley of the passengers on the east of the sea." That is, of Gennesareth, according to the Targum. The valley near this lake or sea is called the Valley of the Passengers, because it was a great road by which the merchants and traders from Syria and other eastern countries went into Egypt; see Genesis 37:17, 25.

"There shall they bury Gog and all his multitude." Some read, "There shall they bury Gog, that is, all his multitude." Not Gog, or Antiochus himself, for he was not in this battle; but his generals, captains, and soldiers, by whom he was represented. As to Hamon-gog, we know no valley by this name. But we may understand the words thus: the place where this great slaughter was, and where the multitudes of the slain were buried, might be better called Hamon-gog, the valley of the multitude of Gog, than the valley of passengers; for so great was the carnage there, that the way of the passengers shall be stopped by it.

Verse 12: "And seven months shall the house of Israel be burying of them." It shall require a long time to bury the dead. This is another figurative expression; which, however, may admit of a good deal of literal meaning. Many of the Syrian soldiers had secreted themselves in different places during the pursuit after the battle, where they died of their wounds, of hunger, and of fatigue; so that they were not all found and buried till seven months after the defeat of the Syrian army.—Adam Clarke.

35

Certainly the overthrow of the forces of Antiochus fits—at least in a general way—the tone of the prophecy under consideration. I do not know, however, that we have history to match every detail that is given. But this is true of other prophecies also—all details may not be spelled out in some secular history available today. Isaiah 16:14 is an example: "Within three years, as the years of an hireling, and the glory of Moab shall be contemned, with all that great multitude; and the remnant shall be very small and feeble." Matthew Henry has pointed out that we have no sacred or secular history that says this happened within three years, yet there is no reason to doubt its historical fulfillment.

The prophecy of Ezekiel 38 and 39 has been called "the most difficult prophecy in the Old Testament." But despite details we may not understand, that interpretation which would place it as a LITERAL battle of the FUTURE seems, to me, the least likely. My reasons for this I will sum up as follows:

If the prophecy of Ezekiel 38 and 39 is future, then huge armies of the world will have to go back to a dependance on horses. Every soldier will ride a horse.

If future, then Israel will have to be at rest, dwelling safely. Cities in other lands will have to build walls around them for protection, so that Israel, in comparison, can be called a "land of unwalled villages."

If future, then major nations will go back to the use of primitive weapons made of wood such as bows, arrows, and spears.

In view of this evidence, if Ezekiel was describing a literal battle, its setting must have been in ANCIENT times. I realize there are good Christian people who may hold a different view. They are at perfect liberty to do so. I would never think of making the interpretation of a prophecy such as this a basis of fellowship. I have presented what I feel is the best explanation, but the reader can make his own decision and be fully persuaded in his own mind.

Chapter 4
JOEL'S PROPHECY
—Future or Fulfilled?

THE OUTPOURING OF THE HOLY SPIRIT on the day of Pentecost, was explained by Peter as a fulfillment of prophecy.

"This is that which was spoken by the prophet Joel; 'And it shall come to pass in the last days, saith God, I will pour out of my Spirit upon all flesh: and your sons and your daughters shall prophesy, and your young men shall see visions, and your old men shall dream dreams: and on my servants and on my handmaidens I will pour out in those days of my Spirit; and they shall prophesy: and I will show wonders in heaven above, and signs in the earth beneath; blood, and fire, and vapor of smoke: the sun shall be turned into darkness, and the moon into blood, before that great and notable day of the Lord come: and it shall come to pass, that whosoever shall call on the name of the Lord shall be saved'." (Acts 2:16-21).

Those who follow the futurist method of interpretation see only a vague connection between what Peter quoted from Joel and what happened at Pentecost. They are prone to believe the real fulfillment will be an outpouring of the Holy Spirit upon the Jews at some future time—a time disjointed from Peter's day by about 2,000 years. In effect, this is saying that Peter quoted this portion out of its proper setting. The implication is that when Peter said, "This is that which was spoken by the prophet Joel," it was not really that!

What about it? Did Peter quote a prophecy which had only a minor connection with the days in which he lived and the real fulfillment is still in the future? Did Peter not know where they were in the divine schedule?

The prophecy of Joel said, "It shall come to pass afterward..." When Peter quoted this portion, instead of "afterward"

37

he used the term "the last days," an expression understood among the Jews as indicating the times of the Messiah. Peter obviously knew the Messiah had come, and these were the very days Joel spoke of, when men could receive of this outpouring from Him who is the baptizer with the Holy Spirit.

Peter also knew that Jerusalem, the temple, and the Jewish nation would be destroyed, as Jesus had explained, within that generation (Matt. 23:36; 24:2, 34). Peter knew it was "the last days" for that city and nation. Either they could receive of this outpouring, or face the judgment pronounced upon the unbelieving portion of that city and nation.

Whatever Peter meant by the expression "last days," he certainly did not think of it as a time 2,000 years from the time at which he spoke. He applied it to what was happening then and there!

As to the expression "all flesh," it is seen within the text that this outpouring would not be limited just to men, but included women; would not be limited to the old, but the young were included also. The Holy Spirit was made available to "Jews, devout men, out of every nation under heaven" (Acts 2:5) who were dwelling at Jerusalem at the time. Ultimately Gentiles also received the same Spirit (Acts 10). This outpouring was not limited to one race, sex, or age group, but was made available to all flesh.

The universality of the gospel is also seen in that portion of the prophecy which said: "And it shall come to pass, that WHOSOEVER shall call on the name of the Lord shall be saved" (Acts 2:21). This certainly does not await a future fulfillment, for the New Testament writers applied these words to the gospel era: "...the same Lord over all IS rich unto all that call upon him. *For* whosoever shall call upon the name of the Lord shall be saved" (Rom. 10:12, 13).

The reason some have supposed Joel's prophecy is future—in spite of what Peter said!—is because it speaks of the sun being darkened, the moon being turned to blood, and "the day of the Lord"! They feel such terms must refer to the very end of this age, to final things. But while the scriptures speak of a final, end-time "day of the Lord" (1 Thess. 5:2), the expression was commonly applied by the prophets to DIFFERENT times in Biblical history, as the following four examples show.

1. EDOM. The destruction that came upon the land of Edom was called "the day of the Lord." The book of Obadiah, as the opening verse explains, was written "concerning Edom." The people of Edom lived in an area naturally well fortified with rocky mountains and cliffs. Yet in spite of their feeling of security, as the context shows, judgment was to come upon them, even as upon the heathen who failed to help Jerusalem in its time of need. "For THE DAY OF THE LORD is near upon all the heathen: as thou hast done, it shall be done unto thee: thy reward shall return upon thine own head" (Obadiah 15).

Edom, also known as Idumea, was given warning by the Lord through Isaiah: "For my sword shall...come down upon Idumea...for it is THE DAY OF THE LORD'S vengeance...from generation to generation it shall lie waste" (Isa. 34:5, 10).

The day of the Lord upon Edom was "NEAR"—not something to take place two or three thousand years later! It was to be destroyed and lie waste FROM GENERATION TO GENERATION—thus not a prediction of the end of time, but long before the end.

An article in the *Dickson Bible* says: "This country...is of very great interest because of the remarkable manner in which the predictions of the prophets have been fulfilled. These predictions portrayed the coming desolation....In the day of its strength and pride it teemed with commercial activity as merchants passed through the land...'None shall pass through it' (Isaiah 34:10)...has been abundantly fulfilled in the cessation of the stream of traffic that in the time of Obadiah passed through that region....In no instance was prophecy more emphatically fulfilled than in the utter desolation of Idumea."[8]

The "day of the Lord" against Edom is long past, fulfilled!

2. EGYPT. Ezekiel prophesied of judgment upon Egypt and certain other nations. "Thus saith the Lord God...the DAY is near, even THE DAY OF THE LORD is near...the sword shall come upon Egypt...I will also make the multitude of

Egypt to cease by the hand of NEBUCHADREZZAR king of Babylon. He and his people with him, the terrible of the nations, shall be brought to destroy the land: and they shall draw their swords against Egypt, and fill the land with the slain" (Ezek. 30:2-11).

Jeremiah said the same: "For this is THE DAY OF THE LORD God of hosts, a day of vengeance....The word that the Lord spake to Jeremiah the prophet, how NEBUCHADREZZAR king of Babylon should come and smite the land of Egypt" (Jer. 46:1-13).

There can be no mistake about it, the "day of the Lord," in this case, was something which took place in the days of Nebuchadrezzar. It was "near" when Ezekiel and Jeremiah prophesied—not something to take place two or three thousand years later.

3. BABYLON. The overthrow of ancient Babylon was called "the day of the Lord." Isaiah wrote: "The burden of Babylon...Howl ye; for THE DAY OF THE LORD is *at hand;* it shall come as a destruction from the Almighty....Behold, the day of the Lord cometh...to lay the land [of Babylon] desolate....Behold, I will stir up the MEDES against them...their BOWS also shall dash the young men to pieces...her time is *near*...her days shall not be prolonged" (Isa. 13:1-22). "The Lord hath raised up the spirit of the kings of the Medes: for his device is against Babylon, to destroy it" (Jer. 50:42; 51:11).

The day of the Lord, in this case, was "near," was "at hand," and would involve the "Medes"—a primitive people—who would fight with bows and arrows. We know from the book of Daniel that the Medes were instrumental in the overthrow of Babylon (Dan. 5:31; 9:1).

Here, then, is another example of "the day of the Lord" in ancient times.

4. JERUSALEM. Zephaniah had given the Lord's message in these words: "I will also stretch out mine hand upon Judah, and upon all the inhabitants of Jerusalem...for THE DAY OF THE LORD is *at hand*...the great DAY OF THE LORD is *near*" (Zeph. 1:4,7,14). Joel, also speaking of Jerusalem and Judah, expressed it this way: "Blow the trumpet in Zion...for THE DAY OF THE LORD cometh, for it is *nigh at*

40

hand" (Joel 2:1). At this time, the temple built by Solomon was still standing as seen by references to the meat and drink offerings, the priests, porch, and altar of the house of the Lord.

We know that the judgment of the day of the Lord which was "at hand" did happen—Jerusalem and the temple were destroyed by the army of Nebuchadnezzar (2 Chron. 36). There would not be another army like this "even to the years of many generations" (Joel 2:2). This wording could not apply to some yet-future and final closing generation, when no more generations would follow!

But how does all of this tie in with the prophecy quoted by Peter on the day of Pentecost? Just this: since the expression "day of the Lord" was used to describe that destruction which came upon Jerusalem in the days of Nebuchadnezzar, it is not unreasonable to believe this same expression could be used to describe the destruction which came upon Jerusalem in 70 A.D. The prophecy that Peter quoted from Joel was not taken out of its proper setting. The outpouring of the Holy Spirit had come, and within a few years judgment—"the day of the Lord"—fell upon that city and nation. All of this is now history.

But, what about the wording, also quoted by Peter, that the sun would be darkened and the moon turned to blood? Would not this refer to the very end of time? No, not necessarily, for similar wording was commonly used regarding events that are now PAST!

Of the destruction of Edom it was said that "all the host of heaven" would "fall down" (Isa. 34:4). Regarding Egypt, "all the bright lights of heaven" would become "dark" (Ezek. 32:7,8; 30:18). Of Babylon, "The stars of heaven...shall not give their light: the sun shall be darkened...the moon shall not cause her light to shine" (Isa. 13:10). And of the destruction of Jerusalem at the time of Nebuchadnezzar, "the sun and the moon shall be dark, and the stars shall withdraw their shining" (Joel 2:10).

In Joel's prophecy quoted by Peter regarding the "last days" of the Jewish era, there was blessing—the Spirit being outpoured—and also warnings of judgment, even divine judgment, the day of the Lord!

Having walked and talked with Jesus, who "opened" to the disciples the true meaning of scripture, Peter was able to

41

recognize the Pentecostal outpouring as the fulfillment of Joel's prophecy. He also knew, from Jesus, that judgment upon Jerusalem would occur within that generation. When, therefore, he quoted the prophecy from Joel about blessing *and judgment*, it was pertinent to the very situation at hand, to that land and people.

The words Peter quoted, about "blood, fire, and vapors [pillars] of smoke," were commonly used to describe warfare in those days. Fighting was done with swords—thus BLOOD was shed. In the process, cities were burned—thus FIRE. With cities being burned, smoke would ascend into heaven—thus PILLARS OF SMOKE. An example of this is found in Judges 20:40: "But when the flames began to arise up out of the city with a PILLAR OF SMOKE...the flame of the city ascended up to heaven."

Josephus' history of the Roman destruction of Jerusalem in 70 A. D. repeatedly uses similar wording: "The Jews seeing this FIRE all about them....this FIRE prevailed during that day and the next also....As the flames went upward, the Jews made a great clamor....a great number fell among the ruins...which were still hot and smoking....At the steps going up to it ran a great quantity of their BLOOD...the FIRE proceeded on more and more....When they saw the FIRE of the holy house...one would have thought that the hill itself, on which the temple stood, was seething hot, as full of FIRE on every part of it, that the BLOOD was larger in quantity than the FIRE, and those that were slain more in number than those that slew them" (Josephus, Wars VI, 4, 5).

The scriptures show that the judgment which fell upon Jerusalem was DIVINE judgment, even though *human* armies carried it out. Thus it was correct to say that *God* did indeed show forth signs of blood, fire, and pillars of smoke.

Bearing these things in mind, and with no straining of argument, we can now see that what Peter quoted was not taken out of its proper setting. He was not speaking words about some other time and place. His words about the sun being darkened and the day of the Lord had a definite message to that generation. When he said: "This is that which was spoken by the prophet Joel," he was not wrong! The time of fulfillment had come!

Chapter 5

THE ONE HUNDRED AND FORTY-FOUR THOUSAND
—Future or fulfilled?

IT IS NOT uncommon for people to believe that the appearance of the 144,000 is something yet to happen in the future. I have met individuals who felt they were called "to train the 144,000." One had purchased property on the desert for this purpose, another a large ranch in the mountains. Back in the early 1950s, a preacher with a large following at the time, taught that he would be instrumental in raising up "144,000 manifested sons of God."

Probably the most popular and widely circulated interpretation at present is that the 144,000 will not make their appearance until during the last seven years of this age. It is claimed that they, like 144,000 "Jewish Pauls," will preach the gospel of the kingdom into all the world—"after the church is gone" in the rapture!

We believe there are serious scriptural objections to this view. Though much of the book of Revelation is given in highly symbolic language, there are two points of identification regarding the 144,000 which should be carefully noted:

1. The 144,000 are taken out of "all the tribes of the children of ISRAEL" (Rev. 7:14).

2. They are "the FIRSTFRUITS unto God and to the Lamb" (Rev. 14:4).

The first point shows their identity. They are Israelites. The term "Israel" is sometimes used in the New Testament in such a way that it includes all believers in Christ regardless of race or national distinction (Gal. 3:29; 6:16). But verses which mention Israel in *contrast* to Gentiles clearly indicate a distinction in terms (Rom. 1:16; 2:9; Acts 13:45, 46). There is such a contrast in the passage before us.

The 144,000 are said to be taken from "all the tribes of the children of ISRAEL" (Rev. 7:4). Then in verse 9 we read: "After this I beheld, and, lo, a great multitude, which no man could number, of ALL NATIONS and kindreds, and people and tongues" who also were redeemed by the Lamb—a vast ingathering from the Gentiles. (The words "Gentiles" and "nations" are translated from the same Greek word—Strong's Concordance, #1484). The 144,000 Christian converts were from Israel; those who followed, the innumerable multitude, were from all nations.

Now according to Revelation 14:4, the 144,000 from the tribes of Israel are "the firstfruits unto God and to the Lamb." The FIRSTFRUITS!

In the Old Testament, the term "firstfruits" designated the FIRST gatherings of the crop which were presented to the Lord (Exod. 23:19; Lev. 2:14; Neh. 10:35). In the New Testament, Christ, who was "the FIRST that should rise from the dead" to immortality (Acts 26:23), is called "the FIRSTFRUITS of them that slept" (1 Cor. 15:20). The FIRST converts that Paul made in Achaia were called "the FIRSTFRUITS of Achaia" (1 Cor. 16:15). And so here, likewise, the 144,000, the firstfruits unto the Lamb, are the first converts to Christ!

Who were the first converts? There can be no mistake about it. The gospel went first to Israelites and THE FIRST CONVERTS WERE FROM ISRAEL!

We believe, then, that the converts from Israel in the early years of the church—back in the first century!—were the firstfruits unto the Lamb and are symbolized by the number 144,000. This fits scripturally and historically. But if the 144,000 have not yet made their appearance, *how* could they possibly be "the *firstfruits* unto the Lamb"? If the 144,000 do not appear until the very last years of this age, it seems more like they would be the *last* fruits.

Let us now briefly review the scriptural evidence that the gospel went first to ISRAEL and that the first converts to the Lamb were ISRAELITES. When John the Baptist introduced Jesus, he spoke of him as "the Lamb of God" and as he who was to be "made manifest to ISRAEL" (John 1:29-31). When Jesus first sent out the twelve, he said: "Go not into the way of the

Gentiles...but rather to the lost sheep of the house of ISRAEL" (Matt. 10:5, 6). Those among the Israelites who believed were filled with the Spirit on the Day of Pentecost. Then three thousand other ISRAELITES were converted on that day alone, men from all the tribes of Israel being represented on that occasion (Acts 2:5, 36). The preaching of the gospel began at JERUSALEM (Acts 1:8; Lk.24:47). The gospel went "to the Jew FIRST" and then also to the Greek (Rom. 1:16).

When Peter spoke to a multitude of Israelites in the temple, he said: "You men of ISRAEL...unto you FIRST God, having raised up his son Jesus, sent him to bless you, in turning away every one of you from his iniquities" (Acts 3:12, 26). Later this same principle was involved in the statement made by Paul and Barnabas to the Jews at Perga: "It was necessary that the word of God should FIRST have been spoken to you: but seeing you put it from you...we turn to the Gentiles" (Acts 13:46).

Nevertheless, there were many thousands of Jews which did receive Christ, so many in fact, that we read in Acts 21:20: "You see, brother, how MANY THOUSANDS [Greek, myriads, or ten thousands] of Jews there are which believe!"

It should be kept in mind also that people of the twelve tribes of Israel were not in areas that were unknown, inaccessible, or lost to the outreach of the early church. Had this been the case, Paul could not have spoken of the "twelve tribes, earnestly serving God day and night" (Acts 26:7).

Converts to Christ came from all the twelve tribes even though they were not all in one area. It was to such converts that James addressed the book which bears his name: "To the TWELVE TRIBES which are scattered abroad" (James 1:1). Also significant is the fact that James refers to these converts as "a kind of FIRSTFRUITS of his creatures" (verse 18), a perfect cross reference to the passage about the 144,000 from the twelve tribes of Israel!

Because there were multitudes of Israelites that were converted to Christ in those early years of the church, it is not unrealistic for these "firstfruits" to be symbolized by the number 144,000. There is no reason to insist on mathematical exactness, however, for the purpose of this symbolic number was probably to contrast with the innumerable multitude whose

45

conversion would follow. Of the converts from Israel, the prophet says: "I heard the number of them." But of the great multitude: "No man could number them" (Rev. 7:4, 9). There is a deep symbolical contrast here—a contrast, however, which fits the facts of history, the greater harvest being from the Gentiles.

In Revelation 14:1 we read: "And I looked, and, lo, a Lamb stood on the *mount Sion,* and with him an hundred forty and four thousand..." One can visit Israel, as I have done, and walk around on the literal hill called mount Sion. But there is a deeper meaning here, for all believers are spoken of as coming to mount Sion, entirely separate from a geographical location!

"You *are* come unto MOUNT SION, and unto the city of the living God, the heavenly Jerusalem...to the church...and to Jesus" (Heb. 12:18-24). These things must be understood spiritually. Having come into a spiritual relationship with Jesus Christ, the 144,000 were pictured as being on mount Sion.

Next, the 144,000 were pictured as having the name of God "written in their foreheads" (Rev. 14:1). References to a name in the forehead occur several times in the book of Revelation. Those who serve the "beast" are said to have his name or mark "in their foreheads" (Rev. 13:16, 17). The "harlot" is seen with a name written upon her forehead (Rev. 17:5). Those who serve the Lord "shall see his face; and his name shall be in their foreheads" (Rev. 22:3, 4).

What is meant by a name in the forehead? Thomas Newton has written: "It was customary among the ancients for servants to receive the mark of their master....These marks were usually impressed on their right hand or on their forehead."[9] Or, in the words of the noted Biblical expositor Albert Barnes, "Among the Romans, slaves were stigmatized with their master's name or mark on their foreheads."[10]

The mark or name in the forehead (as literally used) showed that a person was a SLAVE, and TO WHOM he belonged. Within the symbolic drama of Revelation, those who are slaves of the "Beast" are pictured as having his name or mark in their foreheads; those having God's name in their foreheads, on the other hand, are slaves of the "Lamb." We should not try to make more of this symbol than was intended.

46

Revelation 14:4 tells us that the 144,000 "were REDEEMED from among men." The word "redeemed" has the meaning of purchased, bought. The redeemed are those purchased to God as slaves; they are his servants (in a servitude of love, of course), being "bought with a price"(1 Cor. 7:23).

Being the servants of God, the 144,000 (and also the innumerable multitude) are spoken of as being "before the throne of God" (Rev. 14:5; 7:9). Being his servants they are before the throne to heed his instructions and carry on his work. It is not necessary to think of this position as referring only to the future, or to heaven. The servants of God, even in this life, have access to the throne, to which they are told to boldly come (Heb. 4:16).

We are told that the 144,000 "were not defiled with women, for they are virgins" (Rev. 14:4). It would be a carnal interpretation indeed to say this means only unmarried people. Even Roman Catholic expositors, with their desire to exalt celibacy, do not so read it. All believers are viewed spiritually, as chaste virgins; and as having been presented as such, to Christ (2 Cor. 11:2). They are "without fault" before God (Rev. 14:5) and thus can stand "faultless before the presence of his glory with exceeding joy" (Jude 24), "without blame before him in love" (Eph. 1:4), and as "a glorious church...without blemish" (Eph. 5:27).

Many have supposed that virtually the entire book of Revelation is a prophecy about things that are still future. But this concept completely fails to explain its opening words which say it was written to show the servants of God things "WHICH MUST SHORTLY COME TO PASS" and that the time for their fulfillment was "AT HAND" (Rev. 1:1, 3).

The futurist view about the 144,000 is that they will not be converted until the very last years of this age; whereas the book of Revelation says the 144,000 were the "firstfruits" unto the Lamb! Since multiplied thousands over almost 2,000 years have been converted to Christ, how could a group converted in the future possibly be the firstfruits unto the Lamb?

Some futurists go so far as to say that the church will never be able to preach the gospel into all the world—that this will not be accomplished until "after the church is gone" when, finally, the 144,000 will get the job done!

Strangely enough, what is sometimes an accompanying teaching is that the Holy Spirit (along with the church) will be removed from the earth. One can only question how the 144,000, *without* the Holy Spirit, will be able to do in a few years what the church, *with* the Holy Spirit, did not do in 2,000 years!

What great claims are made for these 144,000 preachers! But where does the Bible ever refer to them as preachers?

In this chapter I have presented what I feel is the best explanation concerning the 144,000. I would stress, however, that the book of Revelation is written largely in symbols. How one interprets symbols, or even what is symbolical and what is not, can lead to different conclusions. On such things I will not be dogmatic. Nor is a study such as this intended for any division or strife. We should take a stand for truth as we come to see it, yet always "endeavoring to keep the unity of the Spirit in the bond of peace...*speaking the truth in love*" (Eph. 4:3, 15).

Chapter 6

THE COMING OF ELIJAH
—Future or Fulfilled?

IN THE WRITINGS of the prophet Malachi, at the very
end of the Old Testament, we read these words:

"Behold, I will send you Elijah the prophet before the
coming of the great and dreadful day of the Lord: and he shall
turn the heart of the fathers to the children, and the heart of
the children to their fathers, lest I come and smite the earth
with a curse" (Mal. 4:5, 6).

What is the meaning of this prophecy? Again, two differing
views emerge: one that the prophecy is still *future*, the other
that it has been *fulfilled*.

According to the fulfilled view, which we believe to be
correct, the prophecy about the coming of Elijah was fulfilled
by the ministry of John the Baptist. This is solidly based on the
words of Christ, who said of John: "If you will receive it, this is
Elijah, which was for to come" (Matt. 11:14). In other words,
though it may have been hard for some to receive, John the
Baptist was the fulfillment of this Old Testament prophecy. He
was the Elijah "which was for to come."

But the evidence does not rest only on this verse. In
another passage, the disciples asked Jesus why the scribes
were saying that Elijah must first come. "And Jesus answered
and said unto them, Elijah truly shall first come, and restore
all things"—quoting Malachi's prophecy. "But I say unto you,
that Elijah IS COME ALREADY, and they knew him not...Then
the disciples understood that he spake unto them of John the
Baptist" (Matt. 17:10-13).

Failing to accept this as final, over the centuries there
have been men who have claimed to be Elijah or have the
Elijah ministry. Many years ago, the Chicago preacher, healer,

49

and founder of Zion, Illinois, John Alexander Dowie, taught that he was Elijah. An interesting and controversial character, with his beard and forceful preaching, he could have well fit the part. But his kingdom fell into discord, after years of preaching against doctors, he was afflicted, divorced by his cousin-wife, and accused of polygamy.

Quite a number of people believed William Branham was Elijah and that his ministry was the forerunner for the return of Christ. He has passed on now. All in all, I suppose there have been several hundred cases in which men have claimed to be Elijah. Such has commonly resulted in misunderstanding and ridicule—all of which could have been avoided by recognizing that John the Baptist, as Jesus explained, had fulfilled the Elijah prophecy.

Now it is true that when John the Baptist began his ministry and was asked: "Are you Elijah?" he answered: "I am not" (John 1:21). He was not the Elijah that had lived many centuries before. The scriptures clearly explain who his parents were and the circumstances surrounding his birth. He was not Elijah in the *literal* sense of the word.

The sense in which John fulfilled the prophecy of Malachi was that he ministered in the spirit and power of Elijah. Before the birth of John, an angel announced: "And many of the children of Israel shall he turn to the Lord their God. And he shall go before him in the spirit and power of Elijah, to turn the hearts of the fathers to the children..." (Luke 1:16, 17). Again, this wording ties in with the Malachi prophecy.

Did John indeed turn the hearts of the fathers to the children? Did he cause many of the children of Israel to turn unto the Lord? Yes, he did. Multitudes were brought to repentance through his ministry (Matt. 3:5, 6). The angel said he would do these things, and he did!

"This is Elijah," Jesus said, "which was for to come." We think the evidence for the fulfilled position is clear. Yet there are those, like Scofield, who say the coming of Elijah prophesied in Malachi is "yet to be fulfilled."[11] Another speaks of "the folly of those who persist in casting aside the precious promise of Malachi 4:5, claiming this auspicious event has already been fulfilled in the person and mission of John, and by such persistence endeavor to overthrow the faith of some."[12] I can only say I do not consider it "folly" to follow what Jesus taught on this. Believing what Jesus taught is not "casting aside the precious promise of Malachi," nor does believing John the Baptist fulfilled the prophecy "overthrow the faith" of anyone.

Because John was not Elijah in a literal sense, there are those who will more or less ignore what Jesus said about John, believing that all prophecy must have a *literal* fulfillment. The following quotation, from a well-known prophecy book, is typical of this thinking: "ALL prophecy about past events has been fulfilled LITERALLY, particularly the predictions regarding the first coming of Christ."[13]

We agree, of course, that many of the prophecies which pointed to Christ's first coming had to do with literal things and events—He would be born at Bethlehem, would heal the sick, speak in parables, be numbered with transgressors, be killed, his bones would not be broken, etc.—but not "ALL" prophecies of Christ's first coming were fulfilled in the LITERAL sense.

Christians recognize Psalm 22 as a prophecy of Christ's first coming and crucifixion, yet LITERAL "bulls" did not attack him, LITERAL "dogs" did not compass him about, nor was he saved from the mouths of LITERAL "lions."

Another example is Psalm 118:22: "The stone which the builders refused is become the head stone of the corner." According to Christ himself, this prophecy found fulfillment in his first coming and rejection (Matt. 21:33-44); but it was not fulfilled in a LITERAL sense!

According to Matthew, Isaiah 42:1 was fulfilled in connection with Christ's first coming: "A bruised reed shall he not break, and smoking flax shall he not quench"(Matt. 12:15-21). Such language prefigured the kindness and mercy of Christ. But the real meaning would not be understood by taking words like "reed" and "flax" in a LITERAL sense.

John referred to Jesus as "the lamb of God" (John 1:29), but Jesus was not a literal lamb.

Jesus said: "I am the good shepherd" (John 10:11), but he was not a keeper of literal sheep. His trade had been carpentry.

51

Jesus said: "I am the door" (John 10:9), but he was not a door in the literal, material sense. He said: "I am the true vine" (John 15:1), but he was not a literal vine. At his first coming, he said: "I am come to send fire on the earth" (Lk. 12:49). This must be understood in a spiritual sense. He did not go about lighting literal fires.

A prophecy closely related to the first coming of Christ had to do with John—as the one who would prepare the way of the Lord: "Prepare the way of the Lord, make straight in the desert a highway for our God. Every valley shall be exalted, and every mountain and hill shall be made low: and the crooked shall be made straight" (Isa. 40:3, 4).

Now the literalist might see in a passage like this modern freeway construction, with mountains being cut down, valleys filled in, and the crooked highway made straight! But turning to Luke 3:2-5, it may be clearly seen this was a prophetic picture of John preparing the way for the appearance of Christ 2,000 years ago. It is highly poetic language that was never intended in a literal sense.

Some even try to use the literal method in interpreting the book of Revelation—a book of *symbols!* What about the "woman" of Chapter 12, clothed with the sun, the moon under her feet, and with 12 stars in her crown? Would any take this to be a literal woman, clothed with the literal sun, and so huge that her feet could reach all the way to the moon? Or what about the great red dragon who takes his tail and casts a third of the stars to the earth? If this is a literal dragon, and the stars are literal stars, how big would it have to be?

The literalist cries: "WE take the Bible just as it reads!"—as though other Christians didn't. Or a statement like, "The Bible means just what it says and says just what it means," sounds good on the surface. But in fact, the Bible often presents truth in veiled language. It uses figures of speech. It uses parables. It uses satire. It uses poetry. It uses types and shadows. It uses symbolism. It uses hyperbole. It uses all of these things—as well as literal statements.

The big question is this: How did Christ and the apostles interpret the Bible? By reading the Old Testament references that they quoted in the New Testament, it is evident they did not follow the literal method of interpretation. If the Old

Testament was to always be taken in the strict literal sense—just as it reads!—it would not have been necessary for Jesus to "open" and explain the real meaning to his disciples (Lk. 24:25-32). Often there was a SPIRITUAL meaning the strict literalist would never grasp.

Being misled by the concept of literal interpretation, the Jews of Christ's day misunderstood much of his teaching. When he said: "Destroy this temple, and in three days I will raise it up," the Jews took this literally. "Then said the Jews, Forty and six years was this temple in building, and will you raise it up in three days?" But Jesus spoke of the temple of his body (John 2:19-21).

Or consider the case of Nicodemus. He was obviously a literalist. When Jesus spoke of being born again, Nicodemus took it literally. "How can a man be born when he is old? can he enter the second time into his mother's womb, and be born?" (John 3:4). But Jesus spoke of a *spiritual* birth.

To the woman at the well, Jesus spoke about water she could drink and never get thirsty again! Thinking in the literal sense, she wanted this water so she would no longer have to make the trip to the well. But there was a deeper meaning; Jesus spoke of spiritual water. Later, when the disciples returned with food, Jesus said: "I have meat to eat that you know not of." Thinking literally, the disciples wondered who had given him food (John 4:14-34).

At the time of our Lord's first coming, the Jews wanted a Messiah who would overthrow the Roman government and set them up as the ruling power in a kingdom of Jewish supremacy. Basing their ideas on a LITERAL interpretation of certain Old Testament prophecies, they supposed Messiah's kingdom would be an earthly, materialistic, political kingdom. But, as we shall see in the chapter that follows, the kingdom which Christ set up was far greater than this—a spiritual kingdom that would ultimately extend to the whole world, not on the basis of race, but grace!

Chapter 7

THE KINGDOM OF GOD
—Postponed or Present?

WHEN JOHN THE Baptist came preaching in the wilderness of Judea, his message was: "Repent: for the KINGDOM OF HEAVEN IS AT HAND" (Matt. 3:1, 2). Jesus also preached: "The TIME is fulfilled, and the KINGDOM OF GOD IS AT HAND: repent and believe the gospel" (Mk. 1:15).

Many Christians think of the kingdom of God as being set up at the *second* coming of Christ. If so, how can we explain Christ's message 2,000 years ago—that the TIME was fulfilled and the kingdom was then and there AT HAND? Was the time really fulfilled or wasn't it? Was the kingdom at hand or was it still 2,000 years in the future?

To answer these questions, there are two basic interpretations that are held by Christians today:

(1) When Christ at his first coming preached that the kingdom was *at hand*, he intended to set up his kingdom at that time. But when the Jews rejected him, he POSTPONED the kingdom and went to the cross. Consequently, the setting up of the kingdom awaits a future day.

(2) The other view, and the one we believe to be correct, also holds that Christ came to set up his kingdom at his first coming. But instead of postponing it, HE DID WHAT HE CAME TO DO. His kingdom was set up, but it was a *spiritual* kingdom, not a worldly, political, Jewish-type kingdom.

To us, the idea that Christ came to set up the kingdom at his first coming, but then had to "postpone" it, is only a theory invented to uphold the literal method of interpretation. The following quotes are representative of Christian teachers who have taught this view:

John Rice: "The Jews rejected Christ their King, and the kingdom was *postponed*."[14]

William Blackstone: "He would have set up the Kingdom, *but* they rejected and crucified Him."[15]

Clarence Larkin: "God...made the attempt to set up His Kingdom on earth," but the Jews rejected it, so "the kingdom has been *withdrawn*" until the second coming.[16]

M. R. DeHaan: "The kingdom of heaven...Jesus offered to the nation of Israel when he came the first time, *but* they rejected it and he went to the cross."[17]

Finis Dake: "Messiah's kingdom...was rejected *so* was postponed until Christ comes to set up the Kingdom."[18]

It is not our intention to cast any reflection upon the sincerity of those who teach this view. But if Christ did indeed come to set up the type of kingdom the Jews expected—but postponed it because they rejected him—we are forced to accept one of two conclusions:

(1) Christ really thought the kingdom was AT HAND and that the Jews *would* accept him when he preached this message—but was MISTAKEN; or, (2) He knew the Jews would *reject* him, that the kingdom would be POSTPONED, and so *wasn't really at hand*—but he went ahead and preached this message anyhow!

Either conclusion is absurd. If Christ was mistaken, then he was not the Son of God. If he was mistaken as to when the kingdom would be set up, how could we know he wasn't mistaken about other things? If he knew the kingdom was still 2,000 years off, but preached that it was at hand, then he was preaching a lie!

But the implications of the "postponement" teaching go deeper still. If the kingdom that Christ offered was the type the Jews expected, and Christ took over as King, then what about Calvary? One writer, seemingly to avoid this point, goes so far as to say: "It can be said at once that HIS DYING WAS NOT GOD'S OWN PLAN. It was conceived somewhere else and yielded to by God. God had a plan of atonement by which men who were willing could be saved from sin and its effects."[19]

I am sure most who hold the postponement teaching would not agree with this statement. Yet, the question remains. If

Christ at his first coming had taken over the kingdoms of this world in the literal sense, there would be no way to fit Calvary into the picture. This would cut into the very heart of the plan of redemption, for without the shedding of Christ's blood in death there would be no remission of sin.

Statements to the effect that "the Jews rejected the kingdom, SO Christ went to the cross," if taken at face value, would imply that Calvary was some last minute arrangement! But the scriptures, such as Isaiah 53, had explained that Christ would die. Without his death, the scriptures could not be fulfilled (Matt. 26:54). He was "delivered by the *determinate* counsel and *foreknowledge* of God" (Acts 2:23). "Those things which God before had showed by the mouth of all his prophets, that Christ should *suffer,* he has so fulfilled" (Acts 4:28). "The prophets and Moses did say that Christ should *suffer"* (Acts 26:22, 23). The death of Christ was the plan of God from the beginning.

The only reason for the kingdom postponement teaching is that it provides a way to hold to the literal method of Biblical interpretation. While it is evidently true that many of the Jews expected a literal kingdom of pomp and political power which would exalt them and put down their enemies, what they thought is not necessarily a sound basis for doctrine. According to Acts 13:27, they did not understand the scriptures. Had they properly understood the scriptures, they would have recognized Christ.

If the kingdom Christ offered was a kingdom of Jewish supremacy with the pomp and glory of David and Solomon—the very thing the Jews wanted—then surely THEY WOULD HAVE ACCEPTED IT. They hated Roman tyranny. On at least one occasion, Jesus purposely escaped so that they would NOT attempt to make him an earthly king! "When Jesus therefore perceived that they would come and take him by force to make him a king, He departed..." (John 6:15).

The Pharisees, who thought of the kingdom as a literal, earthly kingdom that would appear in all the glamor of military might, demanded of Jesus "when the kingdom of God should come" (Lk. 17:20). To this Jesus replied: "The kingdom of God cometh not with observation [outward show]: neither shall they say, Lo here! or, lo there! for, behold, the kingdom of God is within you," or as the margin says, "among you" or "in your midst" (verse 21). The kingdom was not in the hearts of those Pharisees to whom he was speaking, of course; but it was in their midst in the person of the King and his disciples who made up the kingdom which was later established in power on the day of Pentecost.

Christ's kingdom was destined to become far greater than an earthly-type kingdom of Jewish supremacy. Unlike the kingdoms of earth, it was described as "the kingdom of heaven," that is, a heavenly, a spiritual kingdom. It is not called the kingdom *in* heaven, but the kingdom *of* heaven. It is *in* the world, but not *of* the world (John 17:11-16).

Jesus said: "My kingdom is not of this world: if my kingdom were of this world, then would my servants fight, that I should not be delivered to the Jews: but now is my kingdom not from hence" (John 18:36).

Being a spiritual kingdom, it would not advance by the sword or with carnal weapons, but through the preaching of the gospel whereby lives are changed. It would grow gradually over the centuries as the Lord would add to it, and so it did not "immediately appear" (Lk. 19:11) or come "with outward show" (Lk. 17:20).

Jesus said to the Jews: "The kingdom of God shall be taken from you, and given to a nation bringing forth the fruits thereof" (Matt. 21:43). The kingdom was taken from them, and to whom was it given? Jesus said: "Fear not, little flock; for it is your Father's good pleasure to give YOU the kingdom" (Lk. 12:32). The kingdom was given to those who received Christ, not those who rejected him! Peter explained: "But YOU [Christian believers] are a chosen generation, a royal priesthood, an HOLY NATION...which in time past were not a people, but are NOW the people of God" (1 Peter 2:9, 10). It was to this "nation" that the kingdom was given.

Jesus said, "And I appoint unto you a kingdom, as my Father hath appointed unto me; that you may EAT AND DRINK at my table in my kingdom, and SIT ON THRONES judging the twelve tribes of Israel" (Lk. 22:29, 30).

Eating and drinking in the kingdom? There are those who fantasize about a literal, future kingdom with food in abundance, grapes as big as apples, apples as big as watermelons,

57

etc. But in the context of this passage, Jesus had explained the significance of the broken bread and fruit of the vine, and that he would not any more "eat" or "drink" thereof "until it be fulfilled in the kingdom of God" (Lk. 22:16-20). It seems implied, then, that "eating and drinking at his table in his kingdom," could refer to believers coming together to partake of the Lord's supper.

Understanding that Christ's kingdom is a present, spiritual reality, it is not inconsistent to believe that He is spiritually present when believers come to the Lord's table. They are not alone, for as Jesus said, "Where two or three are gathered together in my name, there am I in the midst of them" (Matt. 18:20). He has promised to sup with those who will open the door to him (Rev. 3:20). It is now—within Christ's kingdom —that believers come to the "table of the Lord" (1 Cor. 10:12). The time believers "eat this bread, and drink this cup" is now, showing forth "the Lord's death TILL HE COME" (1 Cor. 11:26)—not something to be done in a postponed kingdom AFTER he comes!

But what about that portion of Luke 22:36 which said the disciples would "sit on thrones judging the twelve tribes of Israel"? Are we to understand this in a spiritual sense also? Since the kingdom is spiritual, we see no reason why positions of spiritual authority may not be intended by these words.

Again, we should look at the context. When the disciples were striving about who would be the greatest in the kingdom, Jesus said: "The kings of the Gentiles exercise lordship over them...but you shall not be so: but he that is greatest among you, let him be as the younger; and he that is chief, as he that serves" (verses 25, 26).

At this time the disciples did not fully understand the spiritual nature of the kingdom—some things not being fully revealed until after the outpouring of the Holy Spirit (John 16:12, 13). But there is the definite implication that their position of authority would be one of humility and not as those who rule over worldly kingdoms.

In a parallel verse, Jesus spoke of them sitting on twelve thrones judging "in the REGENERATION" (Matt. 19:28). In the only other place this term appears, it refers to Christ's redemptive work and the outpouring of the Holy Spirit: "Not by works of righteousness which we have done, but according to his mercy he saved us, by the washing of REGENERATION, and renewing of the Holy Ghost; which he shed on us abundantly through Jesus Christ" (Titus 3:5,6).

Accordingly, the time of regeneration, of new birth, of being born again, is this present age. Jesus said one must be born again to enter the kingdom (John 3:1-8). This was not something that must await the resurrection or a future age, for those who received Christ were given power to become sons of God, "which were born"—born again, born spiritually—"not of the blood, nor of the will of the flesh, nor of the will of man, but of GOD" (John 1:12, 13). Regeneration, being born again, is a present reality. It has been made available through the outpouring of the Holy Spirit.

If, then, the time of the apostles sitting on thrones was to follow Pentecost—the regeneration—then their positions of authority must be understood within the realm of spiritual power, not political power!

If some feel this is going too far, "spiritualizing" too much, we might well compare the fact, as strange as it sounds, that Christians are even called *kings!* "Jesus Christ...loved us, and washed us from our sins in his own blood, and HATH MADE US KINGS" (Rev. 1:5, 6). But this does not mean Christians are kings in the worldly or political sense of the term! They reign in righteousness.

According to the scriptures, the Christian is a soldier (2 Tim. 2:3)—he fights (1 Tim. 6:12)—is in a war (1 Tim. 1:18)—wears armor (Eph. 6:13)—has been given weapons (2 Cor. 10:4)—fights with a sword (Heb. 4:12). All understand these things spiritually. The fight is the fight of "faith," the weapons are "not carnal," and the sword is "the word of God."

In the scriptures, Christians are called soldiers, ambassadors, and kings; servants, sheep, and salt; babes, branches, and bread; a house, building, and temple; lambs, light, and wheat; fishers (of men), workers, and epistles. We all understand these things in a spiritual, non-literal sense. Why, then, should any insist that Christ's words about the twelve sitting on thrones must mean they were to become literal, worldly kings—and then place the whole thing into a postponed kingdom of the future? The power and authority given to believers is spiritual.

In this same sense, Paul spoke of believers as being *seated* with Christ in heavenly places. God has set Christ "at his own right hand in the heavenly places," and has "made us sit together in heavenly places in Christ Jesus" (Eph. 1:2, 3; 2:1-6). Is Christ now seated in the throne of divine authority? Yes. Are Christians seated with him, according to Paul? Yes. Is it not evident, then, that this present position of reigning with Christ must be understood spiritually?

Those who have been seated with Christ have been given spiritual authority. They have the message of the kingdom and its power to bless mankind. They are ambassadors for Christ. They are his representatives. They are his kingdom of kings and priests.

Did the apostles, having this authority, have a ministry to the twelve tribes of Israel? Indeed they did; and, as a result, vast multitudes—from all twelve tribes of Israel—became a part of Christ's kingdom through regeneration, the new birth! The power whereby these men functioned was spiritual power, not political power. They were called to be preachers, not politicians.

Peter was given the "keys of the kingdom of heaven" (Matt. 16:19). Did he use these keys? We believe he did. We believe he used the keys to open the kingdom to 3,000 on the day of Pentecost, for people enter the kingdom by conversion (Matt. 18:3). Later Peter took the gospel to the Gentiles and they too entered in. But if the kingdom had been postponed, then Peter would not have been able to use the keys Christ gave him!

Instead of the kingdom being postponed to the dim, distant future, Jesus said: "Verily I say unto you, That there be some of them that stand here, which shall not taste of death, till they have seen the kingdom of God come with power" (Mk. 9:1). If the kingdom was postponed, some of those people must be getting quite old by now!

The prophet Daniel spoke of the *time* within which the kingdom would be set up. "And in the days of these kings shall the God of heaven set up a kingdom, which shall never be destroyed: and the kingdom shall not be left to other people, but it shall break in pieces and consume all these kingdoms, and it shall stand for ever" (Dan. 2:44).

In a dream, Nebuchadnezzar had seen an image with a head of gold, chest and arms of silver, belly and thighs of brass, and legs of iron with feet of iron and clay. A stone smote the image upon its feet, the whole image was broken up, and the stone became a great mountain filling the whole earth.

The explanation of this dream given by Daniel (see artist's conception of the scene below) indicates that the various parts of the image symbolized four empires: Babylon, Medo-Persia, Greece, and Rome.

The stone cut out without hands represented the kingdom of Christ. It struck into the image of human government in that portion representing the Roman Empire. It seems evident, then, this had to occur while the Roman Empire was still in existence. The time period for the Roman Empire is generally figured from 63 B.C. to 476 A.D. So if it was "in the days of these kings"—the kings who reigned over the Roman Empire —that the kingdom was set up, a time centuries AFTER the days of these kings cannot be the proper meaning.

But did the kingdom of Christ in its clash with the image representing the kingdoms of Babylon, Medo-Persia, Greece, and Rome break in pieces and consume? Yes, it did. But we must keep in mind that it did not conquer, break up, and consume by force and bloodshed. The kingdom of Christ, being spiritual, conquered by spiritual weapons, not by carnal military weapons (2 Cor. 10:4). Men from all parts of the empire were converted. The powers of idolatry were broken up. It was a spiritual victory, not national or political, for Christ's kingdom is not of this world.

Though in adverse circumstances, John spoke of himself as being in the kingdom: "I John, who also am your brother, and companion...*in tribulation,* and IN THE KINGDOM...of Jesus Christ" (Rev. 1:9). John did not believe the kingdom had been postponed. He did not speak of the kingdom as something that would follow a tribulation period of the future. He was in "tribulation" AND in the "kingdom" of Christ—at the *same time!*

Because the kingdom of Christ is an "everlasting kingdom," it is sometimes referred to in a future sense (2 Peter 1:11, etc.). *We do not deny the future aspects of the kingdom.* But this does not annul its *present* reality. With Paul we can say: "The kingdom of God IS..." (Rom. 14:17; 1 Cor. 4:20). RIGHT NOW God hath "delivered us from the power of darkness, and HATH translated us into the kingdom of his dear Son" (Col. 1:13).

As Christians we can rejoice that we are NOW a part of that kingdom and that this kingdom is destined for a glorious and magnificent future!

Chapter 8

CHRIST—KING OF KINGS—NOW!

THE FACT THAT Christ's kingdom is a *present* reality is confirmed by this fact: He is KING *now*. He is not waiting until his second coming to be crowned King of kings. He "IS Lord of lords, and King of kings" (Rev. 17:14). He is now "the King of kings, and Lord of lords, who only hath immortality, dwelling in the light which no man can approach unto" (1 Tim. 6:15, 16).

Jesus is reigning now. God raised him "from the dead, and set him at his own right hand in the heavenly places, far above all principality, and power, and might, and dominion, and every name that is named, not only in this world [age], but also in that [age] which is to come" (Eph. 1:20, 21). This wording should be carefully noticed. His exaltation includes not only the age to come, but THIS AGE AS WELL. He reigns NOW with "all power...in heaven and in earth" (Matt. 28:19). "He is LORD of all" (Acts 10:36).

While it is true that Jesus will come "in his glory" and sit upon his throne as Judge (Matt. 25:31), we must realize that his being glorified in heaven as King has already happened; it does not begin at that time. He "entered into his *glory*" following his death and resurrection (Lk. 24:26). The prophets "testified beforehand the sufferings of Christ, and the *glory* that should follow" (1 Peter 1:11). "God...raised him up from the dead, and gave him *glory*" (verse 21), "both NOW and forever" (2 Peter 3:18). He "was manifest in the flesh...believed on in the world, received up into *glory*" (1 Tim. 3:16) and being exalted in heaven was "crowned with *glory* and honor" (Heb. 2:8, 9).

According to the scriptures, the Holy Spirit was not to be outpoured until *after* Jesus was *glorified*. (John 7:37-39). So the coming of the Holy Spirit on the Day of Pentecost was a sure sign that Jesus had indeed ascended into heaven and been glorified! Thus Peter preached:

"This Jesus hath God raised up, whereof we are all witnesses. Therefore being by the right hand of God EXALTED and having received of the Father the promise of the Holy Ghost, he hath shed forth this, which you now see and hear....Therefore let all the house of Israel know assuredly, that God HATH made this same Jesus whom you have crucified, both LORD and Christ" (Acts 2:32-36).

The word "Lord" used here is from the verb *kurieuo*, which means "to rule,"[20] a term in perfect agreement with the verses in which Christ is called King of kings.

Isaiah prophesied that Christ would be given rulership: "For unto us a child is born, unto us a son is given: and the government shall be upon his shoulder...of the increase of his government and peace there shall be no end, UPON THE THRONE OF DAVID, and upon his kingdom...to establish it with judgment and with justice from henceforth even forever" (Isa. 9:6, 7). Prior to Christ's birth, Gabriel said to Mary: "The Lord God shall give unto him THE THRONE OF HIS FATHER DAVID...and of his kingdom there shall be no end" (Lk. 1:32, 33).

The question before us is this: WHEN was Christ to be exalted to this place of rulership upon the throne of David? Some suppose it is still future. But Peter, speaking on the day of Pentecost, said it had *already happened,* linking it with Christ's resurrection and ascension into heaven!

Peter said that God had promised David "that of the fruit of his loins, according to the flesh, he would raise up Christ TO SIT ON HIS THRONE; he seeing this before SPAKE OF THE RESURRECTION OF CHRIST, that his soul was not left in hell, neither his flesh did see corruption....THEREFORE being by the right hand of God exalted...HE hath shed forth this, which you now see and hear...God HATH made that same Jesus...Lord and Christ" (Acts 2:29-35).

At Pentecost, Peter also referred to another prophecy of David: "The Lord said to my Lord, Sit thou on my right hand, until I make thy foes thy footstool." But this, Peter pointed out, could not have been fulfilled by David, for "he is both dead and buried, and...is not ascended into the heavens." Who, then, was it that had ascended into heaven and was exalted at the right hand of God? It was Jesus Christ! (Acts 2:29, 34-36).

Commenting on this, Curtis Dickinson, a friend of mine for many years, has said: "It is evident that David understood that the Messiah who was to come from his seed would be raised from the dead in order to sit on David's throne while David himself remained in the grave. It is not after the second coming and resurrection of the dead that Christ begins to reign on David's throne, nor is it an earthly throne in the land of Palestine, but it is the heavenly throne of which ancient Jerusalem was only a shadow or type." (*The Witness,* March, 1970).

Those who hold the postponement view say God raised Jesus from the dead so that later—2,000 years or so later!—he would be exalted as King on the throne of David. But this does not fit.

The fact that there will be a resurrection at the last day was commonly believed by the Jewish people (John 11:24). Had Peter been speaking of one taking the throne of David AFTER the resurrection at the last day, the prophecy could then apply to David himself or someone else. His whole argument would have lost its point.

It would be while David still slept with his fathers that Christ would be raised up to sit on his throne. Unless Peter was making statements entirely out of context, there is every reason to believe that Christ fulfilled this prophecy by his resurrection and ascension.

Having ascended into heaven, Christ "sat down on the right hand of God; from henceforth expecting till his enemies be made his footstool" (Heb. 10:12,13). We read also that "he must reign, till he hath put all enemies under his feet. The last enemy that shall be destroyed is death" (1 Cor. 15:25, 26). He must continue to reign until death is destroyed. Since Paul, in this same chapter, says death will be destroyed by the dead being RESURRECTED, it seems clear that the reign of Christ had to begin BEFORE the resurrection of the dead.

Some think the throne of David can only mean a literal, earthly throne in Jerusalem—a rulership over fleshly Jews in a postponed kingdom of the future. But even in the Old Testament era, the "throne of David" was not a term limited strictly to David, but was also called "the throne of the Lord." For example, we read: "Then sat Solomon upon the throne of David

65

his father..." (1 Kings 2:12), and a parallel place says: "Then Solomon sat on the THRONE OF THE LORD as king instead of David his father..." (1 Chron. 29:23).

Peter preached that Christ has been raised from the dead and exalted as King. David's prophecy has been fulfilled in the person of Jesus Christ. David's body saw corruption; he was not raised from the dead to ascend into heaven; his sepulchre was with them to that day. But Christ, while David still slept, has been exalted on his throne. This view brings harmony to the passage and does not require a huge gap or artificial parenthesis of 2,000 years.

But if Christ's exaltation to the throne of David has not occurred—and will not until after the resurrection—Peter's message was simply not relevant. There would be very little, if any, connection between what he preached on the day of Pentecost and what he quoted from the Psalms.

The "throne of David" cannot be limited to a literal throne in Jerusalem, for Christ fulfilled the prophecy by ascending into *heaven* where he was exalted as Lord and Christ. He has "the *key* of David" so that he opens and no man shuts, he shuts and no man opens (Rev. 3:7). No one takes this to mean a literal key, some relic handed down from the days of David.

The same is true regarding the expression "the *tabernacle* of David." By the time James spoke at the Jerusalem council, many Gentiles had been converted. "And to this agree the words of the prophets; as it is written, 'After this will I return, and will build again the tabernacle of David, which is fallen down...that the residue of men might seek after the Lord, and all the Gentiles, upon whom my name is called'." (Acts 15:14-17—quoted by James from the Septuagint version of Amos 9:11, 12).

When James said: "After this," he was QUOTING from an Old Testament prophecy, a prophecy which was future at the time it was given, but not at the time James spoke. What James quoted had reference to that which was then and there taking place: the conversion of the Gentiles!

The "tabernacle" of David, the "key" of David, the "throne" of David, were all understood in a *spiritual,* non-futurist sense by the New Testament writers.

66

According to the futurist point of view, when Peter quoted from Joel and said, "This is that," the portion he quoted was *really* about events to take place 2,000 years later in connection with a postponed kingdom.

Peter said Christ had fulfilled the prophecy about one of David's descendants being seated on his throne. But according to the futurist point of view, when Peter said this, the time for Christ to sit on David's throne was still 2,000 years away when a postponed kingdom would finally be set up!

And, likewise, when James quoted the prophecy about the tabernacle of David in connection with Gentiles being converted, according to the futurist point of view, it had no direct bearing on the subject being discussed.

Were these apostles inspired men? Having been with Christ, having received the Holy Spirit, did they know what they were talking about? I believe they did. They did not interpret these Old Testament prophecies by the so-called *literal* method. They understood them spiritually.

Chapter 9

DISPENSATIONAL DIFFICULTIES

ACCORDING TO THE postponement (dispensational) teaching, when the kingdom was postponed, the GOSPEL of the kingdom was also postponed, to be preached again just prior to the setting up of the kingdom in the future. The following quotes are typical of this view:

> C. I. Scofield: "TWO preachings of this gospel [the gospel of the kingdom] are mentioned, one past, beginning with the ministry of John the Baptist, continued by our Lord and his disciples, and ending with the Jewish rejection of the King. The other is yet *future* (Mt. 24:14) during the great tribulation, and immediately preceding the coming of the King in glory."[21]

> Harry Ironside: "In the gospels, the Lord proclaims the gospel of the kingdom. After the church is taken out, the gospel of the Kingdom will *again* be proclaimed."[22]

> John R. Rice: "The gospel of the kingdom is to be preached *again* during the tribulation period just before Christ returns to set up His kingdom."[23]

> Clarence Larkin: "The gospel of the kingdom is to be preached again...after the Rapture of the Church for a 'witness' unto all nations."[24]

According to the postponement view, during this time when the gospel of the kingdom is not to be preached, we are to preach the gospel of the grace of God. As one writer phrases it, "A remnant of the Jews will preach the Gospel of the kingdom. Today we preach the Gospel of grace."[25] Another says, "The gospel of the kingdom is not being preached now...God called another man, Paul, and revealed to him the gospel of grace."[26]

In a book by C. I. Scofield, the question is asked: "What is the difference between 'the gospel of the kingdom' and 'the gospel of the grace of God'?" Answer: "The gospel of the kingdom is the glad tiding that Christ is to set up his kingdom on earth...the gospel of the kingdom will be the peculiar testimony of the believing remnant during the great tribulation after the church is taken away." But, "the gospel of the grace of God is the glad tiding...that 'God so loved the world, that he gave his only begotten Son'."[27]

Thus a sharp difference is drawn between the "gospel of the kingdom" and the "gospel of the grace of God." But the two terms are actually used *interchangeably* in the scriptures. Paul spoke of preaching "the gospel of the GRACE of God," and in the next verse says he preached "the KINGDOM of God"! (Acts 20:24, 25).

If the preaching of the gospel of the kingdom had been postponed, why was Philip in Samaria "preaching the things concerning the kingdom of God" (Acts 8)? Why was Paul preaching concerning "the kingdom of God" at Ephesus (Acts 19:8)? Why was he at Rome "preaching the kingdom of God" (Acts 28:28-31)? Many references after Pentecost show that the disciples preached the kingdom of God. They knew nothing of a postponed gospel.

When we hear talk of more than one gospel, we are reminded of the words of Paul that there "is NOT another," and "though we, or an angel from heaven, preach any other gospel unto you than that which we have preached unto you, let him be accursed" (Gal. 1:7, 8). The Bible teaches there is ONE gospel, and that one gospel "is the power of God unto salvation to *everyone* who believes"—whether Jew or Greek (Rom. 1:16).

The Bible does refer to the gospel by different terms—"the gospel of the grace of God," "the gospel of God," "the gospel of Christ," "the gospel of our salvation," "the gospel of peace," "the everlasting gospel," and "the gospel of the kingdom"—but this cannot mean there are this many different gospels!

DIVISIONS AT CORINTH

Dispensationalists say we are now to preach the gospel of grace that was revealed to PAUL. We are told that much of what Jesus said pertained to the kingdom and is for another dispensation. We believe the following example will show the inconsistency to which this leads:

The reader will recall that the church at Corinth suffered from divisions. Some were saying: "I am of Paul; and I of

Apollos; and I of Cephas; and I of Christ" (1 Cor. 1:12). In view of this, Paul stressed that they should belong to CHRIST, that CHRIST is not divided, that CHRIST was the one that was crucified, that the others—whether Paul, Apollos, or Cephas —were just men. It was CHRIST who should receive the glory (1 Cor 1:12-15; 3:5-8). The implication is that they were *not* to say, "I am of Paul," or "I am of Apollos," or "I am of Cephas." Instead, their testimony should be: "I AM OF CHRIST." But notice how this is handled in the notes of the Scofield Bible:

"It is evident that the *really dangerous* sect in Corinth was that which said, 'and I of Christ.' They rejected the new revelation through Paul of the doctrines of grace; grounding themselves, probably, on the kingdom teachings of our Lord."[28]

Surely this illustrates how far some will go to promote the theory that Paul's message of grace was a different message than the gospel of the kingdom preached by Christ!

A TRIBULATION REMNANT?

It is quite clear that the *entire* chapter of Matthew 10 was addressed to the twelve disciples. It begins: "And when he had called unto him his *twelve* disciples..." It is followed by these words: "And it came to pass, when Jesus had made an end of commanding his twelve disciples, he departed thence to teach and to preach in their cities."

But Scofield, taking verse 23 entirely out of its setting, supposes it refers to a Jewish remnant during a future tribulation period! "Verse 23 has in view the preaching of the remnant in the tribulation, and immediately preceding the return of Christ in glory. The remnant *then* will not have gone over the cities of Israel till the Lord comes."[29] Thus is the verse arbitrarily removed from its linkage with the first coming of Christ and applied to the second coming!

Jesus told the twelve to go from city to city, and that they would "not have gone over the cities of Israel, till the Son of man be come" (Matt. 10:23). Some translate it: "...until I join you." The simple meaning probably is that Jesus would also be coming to those cities to preach. He had the same arrangement with the seventy who went "before his face into every city and place, whither he himself would come" (Lk. 10:1). The inconsistency of working a futurist view into Matthew 10 should be apparent to all.

KINGDOM OF HEAVEN / KINGDOM OF GOD?

Another feature of the dispensational or postponement teaching is that "the kingdom of GOD" is not the same as "the kingdom of HEAVEN." As early as 1834, John Darby drew distinctions between the terms, a teaching later incorporated into the notes of the Scofield Bible: "The kingdom of God is to be distinguished from the kingdom of heaven."[30] We believe this is arbitrary and unwarranted, for these terms are used INTERCHANGEABLY in the scriptures.

Jesus preached: "The kingdom of HEAVEN is at hand" (Matt. 4:17). The parallel account says he preached: "The kingdom of GOD is at hand" (Mk. 1:15).

The apostles preached "the kingdom of HEAVEN" (Matt. 10:7). They preached "the kingdom of GOD" (Lk. 9:2).

The poor in spirit shall inherit the "kingdom of HEAVEN" (Matt. 5:3). They shall inherit the "kingdom of GOD" (Lk. 6:20).

Many shall come from all directions into "the kingdom of HEAVEN" (Matt. 8:11). They shall come into "the kingdom of GOD" (Lk. 13:29).

The disciples understood the mysteries of "the kingdom of HEAVEN" (Matt. 13:11). They understood the mysteries of "the kingdom of GOD" (Mk. 4:11).

A mustard seed is a symbol of the "kingdom of HEAVEN" (Matt. 13:31). It is a symbol of the "kingdom of GOD" (Mk. 4:30; Lk. 13:18).

The fact is, Matthew generally used the term "kingdom of heaven," while Mark and Luke used the term "kingdom of God." But in Matthew 19:23, 24, BOTH terms are used in the *same* passage! "Verily I say unto you, that a rich man shall hardly enter into the kingdom of HEAVEN. And again I say unto you, It is easier for a camel to go through the eye of a needle, than for a rich man to enter into the kingdom of GOD."

If the "kingdom of heaven" does not mean the "kingdom of God," all of these verses, and others, are very misleading.

RIGHTLY DIVIDING THE WORD?

Dispensationalists commonly quote 2 Timothy 2:15 about "a workman that needeth not to be ashamed, rightly DIVIDING the word of truth" (KJV) as a basis for cutting or dividing the Bible up into various dispensations. But that is not the intended meaning. Notice how it is translated in the following:

"...rightly handling the word of truth" (RSV), "handling accurately the word of truth" (NAS), "who properly presents the word of truth" (Williams), "teaches the word of truth the right way" (Beck), "rightly shapes the message of truth" (Goodspeed), "who correctly handles the word of truth" (NIV), "skillfully handling the word of truth" (Rotherham), "straightforward dealing with the word" (Weymouth), etc.

In context, Paul likened Timothy's ministry to various occupations. He was to endure hardness as a soldier. He was to strive lawfully as one who runs in a race. He was to be a partaker of the fruits as a husbandman. As a workman or builder who does a good job is not ashamed, so Timothy was to be approved to God by rightly preaching the word of truth. He was not to teach errors, as Hymenaeus and Philetus had done (verses 17, 18).

The idea that Paul was telling Timothy to divide or cut up the Bible into dispensations is not even hinted at.

ISRAEL OR CHURCH?

The way some "divide" the word is by teaching that God has a program for the nation of ISRAEL and a different program for the CHURCH. They believe God has an eternal program with fleshly Israel based on promises made to Abraham, a program which was temporarily interrupted at the first coming of Christ when the kingdom was postponed. At the second coming of Christ, they believe, his program with Israel will resume. In the meantime, the church age is presented as a "parenthesis," an age unseen by the Old Testament prophets.

Isn't it true that God promised the land of Palestine to Abraham and his seed forever? Didn't God say that in Abraham's seed all nations would be blessed? Will these promises go unfulfilled? Or will they finally be realized in the age to come?

The promises involving a specific land area and Abraham's fleshly descendants, met their fulfillment within the Old Testament. His descendants were to become a "great nation" (Gen. 12:2)—which they did. They were described as a "GREAT nation" (Deut. 4:6). In verse 7, the question was asked: "For what nation is there so GREAT?"

They were to become a great people—so great that they could not be numbered. The Bible tells us that they did become "a GREAT people" which could not be "numbered nor counted for multitude" (1 Kings 3:8, 9).

They were to become "as the dust of the earth" and as the "stars" (Gen. 13:16; 15:5). This was fulfilled also. Moses said: "The Lord your God HATH multiplied you, and behold, you are THIS DAY as the STARS of heaven for multitude" (Deut. 1:10). They were "a people like the DUST of the earth in multitude" (2 Chron. 1:9) and "many, as the SAND which is by the sea" (1 Kings 4:20). The writer of the book of Hebrews summed it up in these words: "Therefore sprang there even of one [Abraham] ...so many as the STARS of the sky in multitude, and as the SAND which is by the sea shore innumerable" (Heb. 11:12).

Abraham's descendants were to possess the land (Gen. 13:15). This was fulfilled when Joshua took the people into the land of promise: "Behold, I have set the land before you: go in and possess the land which the Lord sware unto your fathers, Abraham, Isaac, and Jacob, to give unto them and to their seed after them" (Deut. 1:8). "And he brought us out...to bring us in, to give us the land which he sware unto our fathers" (Deut. 6:23). "So Joshua took THE WHOLE LAND, according to ALL that the Lord said" (Josh. 11:23). "And the Lord gave unto Israel ALL THE LAND which he sware to give unto their fathers; and they possessed it...there failed not ought of any good thing which the Lord had spoken unto the house of Israel; ALL CAME TO PASS" (Josh. 21:43-45).

According to these verses, they possessed ALL the land that had been promised to Abraham—"all the land of Canaan" (Gen. 17:8). God explained the boundaries and the names of those who then inhabited that land (Gen. 15:18-21). Later, Nehemiah recorded the fulfillment in these words: "Thou art the Lord...who did choose Abram...and made a covenant with him to give the land of the Canaanites, the Hittites, the

Amorites, and the Perizzites, and the Jebusites, and the Girgashites, to give it, I say, to his seed, and HAST PERFORMED thy words" (Neh. 9:7, 8; Josh. 9:1, 2).

As to the promise of possessing the land "forever" (Gen. 13:15), this was clearly based on CONDITIONS of obedience. They were told to keep his commandments, then generation after generation of their people would continually or "forever" dwell in the land. "BUT if thine heart turn away...I denounce unto you this day, that you shall surely perish, and that you shall NOT prolong your days upon the land" (See Deut. 4:40; 30:15-18). It should be understood that the word "forever" used here did not carry the meaning of *eternity*. Things such as circumcision, the passover, the Levitical system, slavery, and fire on the altar were to continue "forever," yet these things only continued within a limited framework (Gen. 17:13; Ex. 12:15; Num. 25:13; Ex. 21:6; Lev. 6:13). That the promise of a continual inheritance of the land was *conditional* is apparent, and that they did NOT continually remain in the land is fact.

Some suppose this tiny portion of land given to Abraham and his descendants is to be the inheritance of Jews throughout eternity. This was not the way the writers of the New Testament understood it. "These all died in faith...they confessed that they were pilgrims and strangers on the earth. For they that say such things declare plainly that they seek a country....But now they desire a BETTER country, that is, an heavenly: wherefore God is not ashamed to be called their God; for he hath prepared for them a city" (Heb. 11:8-12).

Imagine Abraham and his descendants living in the land of Palestine in an age to come and for eternity—and all the time living in disappointment, desiring a BETTER country! It is unthinkable. The literal inheritance of a land area was a mere *type* of greater spiritual realities.

According to the New Testament, the promises given to Abraham find their ultimate fulfillment—not in a small land area—but in JESUS CHRIST AND THE GOSPEL. "Now to Abraham and his seed were the promises made. He saith not, 'And to seeds,' as of many; but as of one, 'And to thy seed,' WHICH IS CHRIST" (Gal. 3:16). Through Christ, all nations were to be blessed by the preaching of the gospel. "And the scripture, foreseeing that God would justify the heathen through faith, preached before the gospel unto Abraham, saying, In you shall all nations be blessed. So then, they which be of faith ARE blessed with faithful Abraham" (Gal. 3:8, 9). The time of all nations being blessed in Abraham's seed is now. It does not await a future, postponed kingdom.

According to the New Testament, Jesus Christ is the promised seed and those who belong to him are the true heirs. "And if you be Christ's then are you Abraham's seed, and heirs according to the promise" (Gal. 3:29). The true seed has come, and "all the promises of God" are IN HIM (2 Cor. 1:20). Outside of Christ the promises are void.

GRACE NOT RACE

At the time of Jesus, there were some who supposed fleshly descent from Abraham made them "God's chosen people." Such was clearly not the case. The natural birth did not count. As Jesus said to Nicodemus, a ruler of the Jews, "You must be born again" (John 3:7). A rebirth, a spiritual birth, was required to enter the kingdom of God.

There was no salvation in the Jews' race or religion. Paul's testimony is proof. He was circumcised the eighth day, of the stock of Israel, of the tribe of Benjamin, an Hebrew of the Hebrews. Yet he had to count all such things as dung, knowing that salvation can be found only in Christ (Phil. 3:5-8).

It has been said: "If Abraham's faith is not in your heart, it will be no advantage that Abraham's blood runs in your veins." John preached to the Jews: "Think not to say within yourselves, 'We have Abraham to our father': for I say unto you, that God is able of these stones to raise up children unto Abraham. And now also the ax is laid unto the root of the trees: therefore every tree which does not bring forth good fruit is hewn down, and cast into the fire" (Matt. 3:9,10).

To those who said, "We be Abraham's seed," Jesus replied: "I know that you are Abraham's seed"—in a fleshly sense. But spiritually, to these same people, Jesus said their father was the *devil!* (John 8:33-44). Think of that!

The fact is, ALL believers in Christ—regardless of race—are Abraham's seed. "If you be Christ's, then are you Abraham's seed, and heirs according to the promise" (Gal 3:29). Those who are of faith are sons of Abraham (Gal. 3:7)

Believers in Christ—regardless of race—are "the Israel of God" (Gal. 6:16). Paul's use of this term could not mean only those converts from fleshly Israel, for Christ has "broken down" the middle wall of partition between and has "made both one" (Eph. 2:14). The entire church is called the Israel of God.

The expression "the circumcision" (Acts 10:45), was a term used in reference to Israelites. "In time past," Gentiles were "called Uncircumcision by that which is called the Circumcision...being aliens from the commonwealth of Israel and strangers from the covenants of promise: but *now* in Christ Jesus you who...were far off are made nigh by the blood of Christ" (Eph. 2:11-14). "For we are the circumcision, which worship God in spirit and rejoice in Christ Jesus, and have no confidence in the flesh"—such as fleshly descent from Abraham (Phil. 3:3).

True believers are "circumcised with the circumcision made without hands, in putting off the body of sins of the flesh" (Col. 2:11)—a statement which can rightly be understood only in a spiritual sense. "For he is not a Jew, which is one outwardly; but he is a Jew, which is one inwardly; and circumcision is that of the heart, in the spirit" (Romans 2:28, 29).

Believers in Christ—regardless of race—are God's chosen people, his nation. In the Old Testament, Israelites were promised they could be a peculiar people, chosen of God, an holy nation (Exod. 19:5, 6). Peter did not hesitate to apply these very words to Gentile believers: "You are a chosen generation...an holy nation, a peculiar people...which in time past were not a people, but are *now* the people of God" (1 Peter 2:9, 10).

Believers in Christ—regardless of race—are called his "sheep." In speaking of that time when Gentiles would come into the fold, Jesus said: "And other sheep I have, which are not of this fold: them also I must bring, and they shall hear my voice; and there shall be ONE fold, and ONE shepherd" (John 10:16). That other sheep would come in and be a part of the same fold with the believing portion of Israel is clearly stated, resulting in one fold and one shepherd over them all, Jesus Christ!

The oneness of God's people—regardless of race—is seen in the illustration given by Paul of an olive tree (Rom. 11:17-24).

Converts from among the Gentiles being grafted in, did not change the tree into another kind of tree. Nor did they form a separate tree. If God had intended to picture Israel as a separate people from the church, there should have been *two separate trees!*

Commenting on this passage, Boettner has well said:

"The people of Israel were the olive tree, but because of unbelief many of them, like dead branches, were broken off....In place of the branches that were broken off, branches from a wild olive tree were grafted in....Thus the life of the olive tree, which is God's people, continues unbroken. Israel and the Christian church are not two distinct olive trees, but one. A clearer illustration of the continuity of Old Testament Israel over into the New Testament church could hardly be imagined."[31]

In the Old Testament, non-Israelites who were allowed to dwell with Israel, were called "the STRANGERS that sojourn among you" (Lev. 17:10, etc.). But now, in Christ, converts from among the Gentiles "are NO MORE STRANGERS...but fellow-citizens with the saints, and of the household of God" (Eph. 2:19).

This oneness in Christ was not fully revealed in the Old Testament. "The mystery of Christ which in other ages was not made known unto the sons of men, *as it is now revealed* unto his holy apostles and prophets by the Spirit; THAT THE GENTILES SHOULD BE FELLOWHEIRS, and of the SAME BODY, and partakers of his promise in Christ by the gospel" (Eph. 3:3, 6). In the Old Testament this was not revealed "as it is now," but this does not mean the church (or church age) was something completely unknown by the Old Testament prophets, for they prophesied "of the GRACE that should come unto you" and of "the sufferings of Christ, and the glory that should follow" (1 Peter 1:10, 11).

According to the New Testament, ALL Christian believers —whether from among the Jews or Gentiles—are called the Israel of God, the elect, an holy nation, the circumcision, the children of Abraham, heirs of the promise, and are all ONE in Christ. The wall of partition has been broken down. What grand truth! What sweeping revelation! What tremendous

PROGRESS! But having accomplished all of this, according to the postponement/dispensational teaching, God will go BACKWARDS and the distinction between Jew and Gentile will again be recognized! "When the church is taken out," says a dispensational writer, "the distinction between Jew and Gentile will be recognized once more."[32]

What? Having established a plan whereby converts from among the Jews and Gentiles have been made ONE, why would God build again "the middle wall of partition" which has been "broken down"? Having brought his sheep—from among Jews and Gentiles—into "ONE fold," will his plan for the future involve TWO folds? Will God end up with two separate and different people—one a heavenly people (the church) and the other an earthly people (the Jews)? Having grafted believers from the Gentiles into the very SAME "tree" with believers from Israel, will he separate them into different trees? Is the New Testament church—in which both have been made ONE —a mere "parenthesis" in God's program?

The answer is summed up well in the words of Boettner: "Ritualism and legalism came to an end with the crucifixion of Christ, and salvation was made equally available for all nations and races. The New Testament age or Church age is therefore no parenthesis, no side issue, but the original divine purpose to which the Old Testament had led step by step."[33]

Chapter 10

DO THE SCRIPTURES TEACH A
JEWISH-TYPE MILLENNIUM?

CHRISTIANS WHO FOLLOW the *literal* method of interpretation, commonly envision a Jewish-type kingdom with
Jerusalem as the world capital and center for a restored temple
worship in the age to come. The outline of future events,
according to this position, is as follows:

When Christ returns, his feet will stand upon the mount of
Olives. Having all the saints with him, he will come to the
eastern gate of Jerusalem. Though sealed up for centuries, it
will be opened for him to pass through into the city. He will
then enter a building, sit on a throne, and be crowned king.
His kingdom, an earthly and political kingdom—postponed
from his first coming—will then be set up. The saints will rule
and reign with him in Jerusalem, which will become the world
capital. The nations will quit fighting—will beat their swords
into plowshares, their spears into pruninghooks. They will
come up to Jerusalem to keep the feast days, new moons, and
sabbaths. An elaborate temple will be built in which a Levitical
priesthood will offer animal sacrifices and carry out the rituals
of the Mosaic system.

It is not my purpose to "throw stones" at any who sincerely
believe this way. I understand. I, too, once believed many of
the points on this outline. I supposed that the evidence for
such a new world coming, a Jewish-type millennial age, was
conclusively given in the scriptures. But as my study continued, certain insurmountable problems with this view became
evident.

I came to realize this concept was based on OLD TESTA-
MENT scriptures. *Not one* of the New Testament writers ever
spoke of Jerusalem becoming the world's center for worship.
Not one New Testament writer ever spoke of Jerusalem as

becoming the world capital in an age to come. When some, today, would make such things major doctrines, was not this quite an omission on the part of the New Testament writers?

Then, too, there was the problem of room. If the resurrected saints of the ages were to all come with Christ into Jerusalem and there crown him king upon David's throne, how would there be room for all of them? Where would everyone stay? Would such a crowded and congested city be glorious?

Not only this, but a literal interpretation of these Old Testament prophecies would even have people coming from all nations riding to Jerusalem on horses, mules, in ox carts, and the like! Could such primitive means of transportation really fit a glorious age of the future?

And then, there was the question of animal sacrifices. As I read these Old Testament passages which spoke of Jerusalem being exalted as a center of worship, several times ANIMAL SACRIFICES were included! Yet, according to the New Testament, the sacrifice of Christ upon Calvary was the PERFECT and FINAL sacrifice for sin! If the age to come will be a return to the old rituals and sacrifices that were abolished by Christ, would not this be RELIGION IN REVERSE? Does God walk BACKWARDS? Thus did I question.

Let us, then, take a look at these Old Testament passages which have been used to teach a Jewish-type millennium.

The outline begins by placing the second coming of Christ in Zechariah 14—"his feet shall stand in that day upon the mount of Olives"—and the verses that follow are taken as a description of a millennial age in Jerusalem. But can the picture presented in Zechariah 14 possibly fit the time of the second coming of Christ? Mention is made of all nations coming against Jerusalem to battle, but they are plagued with a disease affecting their flesh, eyes, and tongues; "AND so shall be the plague of the HORSE, of the MULE, of the CAMEL, and of the ASS, and of all the beasts that shall be in these tents, as this plague" (Zech. 14:15).

Are we to believe that at the time of the second coming of Christ people will have gone back to a dependance upon horses for transportation? If all nations were to make war against Jerusalem, would they be riding on mules or camels? THE

PICTURE GIVEN BY ZECHARIAH IS NOT A PICTURE OF MODERN TIMES!

Not only Zechariah 14, but other Old Testament passages which are quoted as proof texts for a Jewish-type millennium speak of PRIMITIVE forms of travel. Isaiah 66:20 speaks of Israelites from all nations coming to worship, riding "upon horses, and in chariots, and in litters, and upon mules, and upon swift beasts, to my holy mountain Jerusalem."

We believe the setting for these things was within the Old Testament era.

When the people had returned from Babylon, Zechariah encouraged them to rebuild the temple, which they did. Among those prophecies, they were told that "there shall come people, and the inhabitants of many cities: and the inhabitants of one city shall go to another, saying, Let us go speedily to pray before the Lord, and to seek the Lord of hosts....Yea, many people and strong nations shall come to seek the Lord of hosts in Jerusalem, and to pray before the Lord" (Zech. 8:20-22).

People did come up to Jerusalem from the nations. Even at the time of the book of Acts, we read about men of all nations coming to Jerusalem for the day of Pentecost (Acts 2) and of a government official from Ethiopia who came to Jerusalem to worship (Acts 8).

But if we apply such things to an age to come—with multitudes of resurrected people and living nations—such crowds riding into Jerusalem on horses and mules would only add to the congestion of a city filled with animals and people, not to mention the resulting sanitation problem. Are we to believe, as the literal interpretation would require, that people will go to Jerusalem from all nations—places like South America, the United States, and Australia—riding on horses and mules?

FEAST DAYS IN JERUSALEM?

It should be noticed also, within these passages quoted to support a Jewish-type millennium, there are verses about people going to Jerusalem to keep the new moons, feast days, and sabbaths. "And it shall come to pass, that every one that is left of all the nations which came against Jerusalem shall even go up from year to year to worship...and to keep the feast of

81

tabernacles" (Zech. 14:16). "From one new moon to another, and from one sabbath to another, shall all flesh come to worship before me, saith the Lord" (Isa. 66:20-23).

Any literal application of such prophecies, instead of being future, tends to fit more within the OLD TESTAMENT era. The New Testament teaches that such observances were mere shadows of the reality which was to come in Christ: "Let no man therefore judge you in meat, or in drink, or in respect of an holy day, or of the new moon or of the sabbath days: which are a shadow of things to come, but the body is of Christ," or as the Goodspeed version says: "That was all only the SHADOW of something that was to follow; the REALITY is found in Christ" (Col. 2:16, 17).

The idea that men must go to Jerusalem in a future age to worship the Lord is contrary to what Jesus taught. Realizing the limited capacity of a LOCALIZED worship, and looking forward to the UNIVERSAL scope of the gospel, he said: "The hour cometh, when you shall neither in this mountain NOR YET AT JERUSALEM, worship the Father...God is a Spirit: and they that worship him must worship him in spirit and in truth" (John 4:20-24).

If it is true that men may now worship God wherever they are, are we to suppose that God will go BACKWARDS and require that men once again go to Jerusalem to worship him? Are we to believe that God will go from the universal back to the local? If so, the words of Jesus were certainly misleading when he revealed the universal worship of the Father.

HEATHENISTIC WORSHIP IN ANCIENT TIMES

When passages speak of ancient heathen rites, which are no longer practiced, their *historical* setting is strongly implied. Take Isaiah 66:15-17, for example: "For, behold, the Lord will come with fire, and his chariots like a whirlwind, to render his anger with fury, and his rebuke with flames of fire....They that sanctify themselves, and purify themselves in the gardens behind one tree in the midst, eating swine's flesh and the abomination, and the mouse, shall be consumed together." Expressions about the Lord coming with fire, chariots, etc., were commonly used to describe God's judgments, even though they were carried out by heathen armies (Jer. 4:13; Ezek.

22:31; etc.). This passage cannot refer to the second coming of Christ, for the forms of worship described were ANCIENT rites that are no longer practiced. The references about eating swine's flesh and the mouse are not speaking of mere diet, but were done in connection with heathenish worship, as the context shows.

In the chapter before, even some Israelites were among those who took part in this heathenish worship—people "that sacrifice in gardens, and burn incense upon altars of brick; which remain among the graves, and lodge in the monuments; which eat swine's flesh, and broth of abominable things is in their vessels...which have burned incense upon the mountains" (Isa. 65:3-7). These superstitious rites, involving witchcraft and necromancy, are not practiced by Israelites today. Because of this, such passages hardly seem to be a picture of events at the time of the second coming of Christ.

PRIMITIVE WEAPONS

Also, passages such as Isaiah 66 can hardly fit our day (or the future), for they speak of *ancient* nations and their use of PRIMITIVE weapons. "I will send those that escape of them unto the nations, to TARSHISH, PUL, and LUD, that draw the BOW..." (Isa. 66:19). Nations today do not fight with bows. Isaiah spoke of nations beating their "swords into plowshares, and their spears into pruninghooks" (Isa. 2:4). If these terms are taken literally, the setting would have to be when such weapons were in use.

FEEBLE PEOPLE IN AN AGE TO COME?

Passages that are sometimes quoted in support of a Jewish-type millennium picture people so old and feeble they would need walking sticks to help them get around! "I am returned unto Zion, and will dwell in the midst of Jerusalem: and Jerusalem shall be called a city of truth; and the mountain of the Lord of hosts the holy mountain....There shall yet OLD MEN and OLD WOMEN dwell in the streets of Jerusalem, and every man WITH HIS STAFF IN HIS HAND FOR VERY AGE. And the streets of the city shall be full of boys and girls playing in the streets thereof" (Zech. 8:3-5).

This is no picture of a FUTURE golden age. Zechariah prophesied at the end of the seventy years captivity in Babylon

(Zech. 1:12). He prophesied unto the Jews who had returned, to encourage them to "build the house of God...at Jerusalem" (Ezra 5:1, 2). Their temple had been destroyed by Nebuchadnezzar many years before, their city had been desolate, and they had been captives. But now—now they had returned and God's blessing had returned to them! "Thus saith the Lord; I am jealous for Jerusalem and for Zion...I AM RETURNED to Jerusalem with mercies: my house shall be built in it...the Lord shall yet comfort Zion, and shall yet choose Jerusalem" (Zech. 1:14,17).

When the Lord said, "I am returned," this was not a prophecy about the second coming of Christ and a millennium to follow. So also, in Zechariah 8, the Lord said: "I AM RETURNED...and will dwell in the midst of Jerusalem." There would be old people, and every man with his staff in his hand for age. This had to do with the condition of things following the return from the Babylonian captivity. We should not wrest such passages from their obvious setting and try to apply them to a future age.

MARRIAGE IN THE AGE TO COME?

Some have thought of the age to come as a time when people will get married and produce children in abundance. They quote the verse about Jerusalem being "full of boys and girls playing in the streets thereof" (Zech. 8:5). Or, "They shall not labor in vain, nor bring forth for trouble; for they are the seed of the blessed of the Lord, and their offspring with them ...The wolf and the lamb shall feed together, and the lion shall eat straw like the bullock....They shall not hurt nor destroy in all my holy mountain" (Isa. 65:23-25). Some believe that priests who serve in a "Millennial Temple," as they call it, will get married (Ezek. 44:22) and that non-Israelites also will "beget children" (Ezek. 47:22).

But this was not the way Jesus interpreted these Old Testament passages! He taught that the age to come would NOT be a time of marriage and, consequently, not a time of abundant births. "The children of this world marry and are given in marriage," he said, "but they which shall be accounted worthy to obtain that world, and the resurrection from the dead, neither marry, nor are given in marriage" (Lk. 20:34, 36). Those who obtain that world—that world following the resurrection, that age to come—do not marry. In view of this, we do not envision the world to come as a time of multiplied births and an ever increasing population.

JERUSALEM AS A PLACE TO LIVE

If Jesus returns to earth and lives in Jerusalem, his words about "where I am, there you may be also" (John 14:3) have been taken to mean that Jerusalem will also be the main place of residence and assembly for the saints.

But just how desirable would it be to live in Jerusalem in such crowded conditions? How would all the redeemed fit into the small compass of that literal, earthly city? Are we to believe that Christ will start some vast remodeling program, fixing up old buildings, making them suitable for occupancy or perhaps order the construction of some huge condominiums in which the saved will live?

None of the apostles ever preached that the city of Jerusalem would be the residence of the saved in an age to come. What glory would there be in this? Men like Peter—and the other apostles—WERE ALREADY LIVING THERE! Surely their hope was greater than a mere geographical location of such limited scope.

The idea that the redeemed of the ages will live in the literal, earthly city of Jerusalem is like saying all the people of a large city would live in one room of a small house. Such would not only be undesirable, it would be impossible.

Were any of us really thrilled about living in old Jerusalem? Did we really want to ride a mule or camel to the temple to worship? Did we really want to depend on an ox-cart for transportation for 1,000 years? Did we really want to walk around with a staff in our hand? I can only say that God's plan is much greater in scope than the confines of a mere city, or country, or even the world itself. His plan involves the whole universe!

THE "EAST GATE" OF JERUSALEM

There is a gate in the eastern wall of Jerusalem which has been closed up since the year 1530 A.D. Some teach it will finally be opened for Christ to pass through into Jerusalem at his second coming. Typical of this viewpoint is the following

85

statement from a widely read religious magazine: "Across from the Mount of Olives is the East Gate of Jerusalem. It has been sealed for centuries as Ezekiel predicted, and will remain so until the Messiah's return. It is through the East Gate, the prophets say, that Jesus Christ will enter."

However, only a very little investigation is required to determine that: (1) the gate Ezekiel mentioned has nothing to do with the present gate referred to by this name in Jerusalem, and (2) the "prince" that Ezekiel mentioned is not Jesus Christ.

"This gate shall be shut, it shall not be opened, and no man shall enter in by it...it is for the prince"—said Ezekiel (Ezek. 44:1-3). But this gate was "the gate of the outward SANCTUARY which looketh toward the east." It was a gate linked with a TEMPLE in Ezekiel's vision—not the gate in an old wall of present-day Jerusalem! The measurements and details are not the same (Ezek. 40:6-16).

To believe that the "prince" that would pass through this gate is Jesus Christ—and that at his second coming—is even more inconsistent. Notice what Ezekiel says about this prince:

"And it shall be the prince's part to give burnt offerings, and meat offerings, and drink offerings...he shall prepare the sin offering...to make reconciliation for the house of Israel" (Ezek. 45:17). Imagine Jesus—after paying the full price for sins at Calvary—coming back and offering such things as animal sacrifices to make reconciliation! In the light of the New Testament, this cannot be. Christ has already made reconciliation for Israel—and the whole world as well!

But notice further. Not only was this "prince" of Ezekiel's vision to offer animal sacrifices for others, but for HIS OWN SINS as well! "And upon that day shall the prince prepare FOR HIMSELF and for all the people of the land a bullock for a SIN offering" (Ezek. 45:22). This could not refer to Christ, for he "needeth not daily, as those high priests, to offer up sacrifice, first for his own sins, and then for the people's" (Heb. 7:27). Christ did not sin (1 Peter 2:22).

Ezekiel explained WHEN the gate was to be shut—during the six working days and opened on the sabbath and new moons for the prince (Ezek. 46:1, 2). Nothing is said about a gate being shut for centuries!

To apply such references in Ezekiel to Jesus Christ—in a literalistic way—is very strained. Nevertheless, people who ought to know better keep talking about the sealed up East Gate just waiting for the Messiah to come, open it up, and pass through it like Ezekiel predicted! It makes an interesting story for guides to tell on holy land tours.

EZEKIEL'S TEMPLE—IS IT FUTURE?

What, then, is the meaning of the temple with which this gate was associated in the closing chapters of Ezekiel?

Adam Clarke says this temple was probably that which Ezekiel saw before the captivity, and which had been burned by the Chaldeans. On comparing the book of Kings and Chronicles with the prophet, we find the same dimensions in the parts described by both (cf. 1 Kings 6:3-16 with Ezekiel 41:2, etc.). The inside ornaments of the temple are entirely the same; in both we see two courts, an inner one for the priests, and an outer one for the people (cf. 1 Kings 4:29-36; 2 Chron. 4:9; and Ezek. 41:16, 17 and 48:7-10). So there is room to suppose that, in all the rest, the temple of Ezekiel resembled the old one; and that God's design in retracing these ideas in the prophet's memory was to preserve the remembrance of the plan, the dimensions, the ornaments, and the whole structure of this Divine edifice, so that at their return from captivity the people might more easily rebuild it.[34]

If the temple built after the captivity failed to fully measure up to the grand scale of the prophecy, it could be a total fulfillment was conditioned on a total obedience: "...let them measure the pattern. And IF they be ashamed of all that they have done, show them the form of the house, and the fashion thereof" (Ezek. 43:10, 11). Others feel the closing chapters of

Ezekiel, though written in all the detail and imagery of the Old Testament, are best understood in a spiritual sense. But whatever may be the correct interpretation, there are very strong reasons for rejecting that which would make this a literal temple of the future:

1. IF EZEKIEL WAS DESCRIBING A LITERAL TEMPLE AND WORSHIP OF THE FUTURE, IT WOULD MEAN A RETURN TO THE RITUALS OF THE OLD TESTAMENT. Priests would have to observe the elaborate ritual of changing garments (Ezek. 44:19). They would wear only linen, linen bonnets and linen breeches—no wool (Ezek. 44:17, 18). Only priests could approach the holy place (Ezek. 42:13, 14). Since the New Testament pictures ALL believers as now having access to God (Heb. 10:19, 20), and ALL being a part of a "royal priesthood" (1 Peter 2:9), a return to a limited priesthood and the rituals of the Mosaic system would be going BACKWARDS.

2. IF EZEKIEL WAS DESCRIBING A TEMPLE AND WORSHIP WHICH PERTAINS TO AN AGE TO COME, IT WOULD BE AN AGE OF PEOPLE GETTING MARRIED. Priests would marry, but could not marry widows, unless they were widows of other priests (Ezek. 44:22, 25). Can Christians really believe this refers to a priesthood following the resurrection of the dead? Jesus himself said those who obtain the world to come are not given in marriage (Lk. 20:34, 36). Besides, if Ezekiel was describing conditions after the resurrection, how could a priest marry the "widow" of another priest? If this was after the resurrection—if her husband was raised from the dead—*she would not be a widow any more!*

3. IF EZEKIEL WAS DESCRIBING A LITERAL TEMPLE AND WORSHIP OF THE FUTURE, IT WOULD MEAN A RETURN TO CIRCUMCISION. The reader should carefully notice that Ezekiel's message cannot be limited to circumcision of the heart. It plainly says: "No stranger, uncircumcised in heart, nor uncircumcised IN FLESH, shall enter into my sanctuary" (Ezek. 44:9). If fleshly circumcision will be a religious requirement in the future, then the New Testament message that "in Jesus Christ neither circumcision availeth anything, nor uncircumcision; but faith which worketh by love" (Gal. 5:6) would have absolutely no valid meaning.

4. IF EZEKIEL WAS DESCRIBING A LITERAL TEMPLE AND WORSHIP OF THE FUTURE, THEN ANIMALS WILL AGAIN BE OFFERED AS SACRIFICES FOR SIN! Priests would slay the burnt offering, the sin offering, and the trespass offering (Ezek. 40:38, 39) and sprinkle the blood on the altar (Ezek. 43:18). "Seven days shalt thou prepare every day a goat for a SIN offering; they shall also prepare a young bullock, and a ram out of the flock...the priests shall make your burnt offerings upon the altar...and I will accept you, saith the Lord" (Ezek. 43:25, 27). "Thou shalt daily prepare a burnt offering unto the Lord of a lamb" (Ezek. 46:13) and by sacrificing lambs, "reconciliation" will be made for the people (Ezek. 45:15).

Is it necessary to point out that all of this, if intended for some future temple, is absolutely and utterly contrary to the teachings of the New Testament? When men have already been "RECONCILED to God by the death of his SON" (Rom. 5:10), what possible purpose could there be to offer lambs every day in some future age? The sacrifice of Christ was the *final* and perfect sacrifice for sins (Heb. 9:12, 26; 10:4-12).

The message of the apostles was clearly that the old covenant with its "gifts and sacrifices...meats and drinks, and divers washings, and carnal ordinances" (Heb. 9:9, 10) has been replaced by the new covenant. Christ is "the mediator of a better covenant...a NEW covenant...he hath made the first old" (Heb. 8:6-13). The old covenant "is done away" and "abolished" (2 Cor. 3:6-13). The new covenant, through his blood, is an "everlasting covenant" (Heb. 12:24).

The New Testament writers taught there could be no going back to Judaism or a mixture of Judaism. Those who advocated such were termed "false brethren" who bring people into "bondage" instead of the liberty of Christ (Gal. 2:3-5). Paul asked: "How turn you again to the weak and beggarly elements, whereunto you desire again to be in bondage?" (Gal. 4:9). "For if I build again the things which I destroyed, I make myself a transgressor...if righteousness is by the law, then Christ is dead in vain" (Gal. 2:18-21).

If a return to the Mosaic system in this present age cannot make any righteous, then it is certain that righteousness cannot come through such in an age to come.

89

According to Christadelphian booklets, a tremendous earthquake will elevate Mount Zion as seen in the accompanying drawing, the summit of which will serve as a massive altar where people from all over the world will bring animals to be killed in sacrifice in the age to come.[35] It would appear from the drawing that so many sacrifices will be offered that the sky will be filled with smoke.

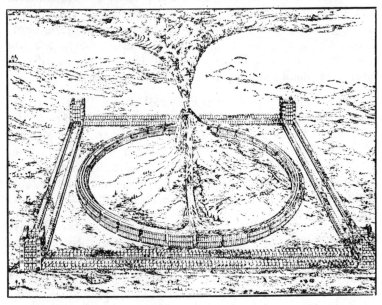

But according to the scriptures, this cannot be. Animal sacrifices did not take away sin in the Old Testament, and there is no way they can serve any purpose in the future (Heb. 10:4, 11)—as "memorials" or otherwise. So let the ovens that bake meal offerings now be cooled. Let the sacrificial animals go back to pasture. Let the blood dry on the horns of the altar. Christ's work of atonement is a finished work!

Can any really be thrilled at the idea of a future temple with animals continually being killed and altars streaming with blood? Would this be glorious? Even though temple attendants might do their best to clean away the blood and filth, imagine the stench of this slaughter house with sacrifices continually being made! Are we to believe that such a temple will be the center for the world's worship in a Golden Age to come? This would be *religion in reverse!*

A SPIRITUAL TEMPLE

The veil of the old temple was torn in two (Matt. 27:51), showing God's presence and blessings upon it were over. In place of that temple, God raised up a *people* who, themselves, became the temple of God, having been filled with his Holy Spirit on the day of Pentecost. Thus Paul could say to believers: "YOU are the TEMPLE of the living God; as God has said, I will dwell in them" (2 Cor. 6:16). "YOU...are built upon the foundation of the apostles and prophets, Jesus Christ himself being the chief corner stone; in whom all the building fitly framed together grows unto an holy TEMPLE in the Lord" (Eph. 2:19-22). Christians are the HOUSE of God (1 Peter 4:17). "YOU, as lively stones, are built up a spiritual HOUSE" (1 Peter 2:5). Within God's spiritual temple, the church, Christians are "an holy priesthood" and they "offer up spiritual sacrifices" (1 Peter 2:5)—sacrifices such as praise, giving thanks, and doing good (Heb. 13:15, 16).

Having raised up a SPIRITUAL temple, will God go back to a carnal temple and animal sacrifices? It cannot be. The New Testament evidence against such is overwhelming and conclusive.

REVELATION TWENTY

Revelation 20, of course, mentions a "thousand years," a period commonly called the millennium. However, some things have been read into this chapter which are simply not there.

As an act in a drama, the scene in Revelation 20 gives a word-picture description of an angel coming down from heaven who binds the dragon (the Devil) with a chain, and throws him into a bottomless pit. The language is highly symbolic. The "chain," for example, could not be a literal chain. Such fetters did not bind the man possessed of devils (Mk. 5:4), how much less could they bind the Devil himself!

The dragon is bound "one thousand years" and does not deceive the nations any more until the thousand years are fulfilled. After this he is loosed a little season, goes out to deceive the nations, and gathers them to battle. We read of those who are beheaded for the witness of Jesus, who do not worship the beast, who are seated upon thrones, who live and reign a thousand years. We read of the first resurrection and that the rest of the dead live not until the thousand years are finished. This is a summary of the scene in Revelation 20.

Nothing is said about a rebuilt temple in Jerusalem; nothing about people coming to Jerusalem in order to worship; nothing about Christ reigning in Jerusalem; nothing about animal sacrifices!

The Bible speaks of an age or world to come (Heb. 6:5), and even uses the term "ages to come" (Eph. 2:7). But it is not our purpose here to attempt a detailed exposition regarding a-millennialism, post-millennialism, or pre-millennialism, in which we would argue one viewpoint against the other. Each of these systems of interpretation has its able defenders. Each has its own arguments. To us, the main issue is not so much *where* we place the millennium in relation to other events, but *what* we place IN this millennium. This makes the difference.

According to the New Testament, there can be no going back to those things which have been abolished through Christ. A return to the Mosaic system with its temple and sacrifices would reverse the proper order of events, would carry us backward from the substance to the shadow, from the reality to the type, from the spiritual to the carnal, from the blood of Christ to the blood of bulls and goats, from the new covenant to the old covenant, from the new Jerusalem to the old Jerusalem, from the better hope to that which made nothing perfect, from the perfect gospel to the yoke of bondage, from Jesus to Moses, from Christianity to Judaism!

Chapter 11

ZECHARIAH FOURTEEN
—Future or Fulfilled?

MANY OF US HAVE supposed that Zechariah 14 is a prophecy regarding the time of the second coming of Christ. Yet, the picture it gives is of a time when nations would be depending on primitive means of transportation—mules, horses, and camels. This does not fit modern times.

The chapter begins: "Behold, the day of the Lord cometh," wording that is sometimes linked with the second coming of Christ. However, the expression "day of the Lord" is also used in the Bible of some events that are now history (see pp. 38-41).

Mention is made of nations coming against Jerusalem to battle, that half of the city would go into captivity, and "then shall the Lord go forth, and fight against those nations, as when he fought in the day of battle" (Zech. 14:3). But again, this does not require a future fulfillment, for similar wording was used in the Old Testament of battles which are now past (Deut. 1:30; 3:22). "The Lord God fought for Israel" in the day of battle (Josh. 11:42). In such cases, he granted victories for Israel, but it did not involve his bodily presence.

The statement, "The Lord shall be king over all the earth" (Zech. 14:9) is also an expression used in the Old Testament when Jerusalem and Israel enjoyed God's favor: "For the Lord IS a great King over all the earth" (Psalms 47:2).

Even the phrase "and the Lord my God shall come, and all the saints with thee" (Zech. 14:5), does not necessarily require fulfillment at the second coming of Christ, for similar wording was used of an event that happened in the Old Testament: "The Lord came from Sinai...he came with ten thousands of saints: from his right hand went a fiery law for them" (Deut. 33:2).

But what about Zechariah 14:4? "And his feet shall stand in that day upon the mount of Olives, which is before Jerusalem on the east, and the mount of Olives shall cleave in the midst thereof toward the east and toward the west, and there shall be a very great valley; and half of the mountain shall remove toward the north, and half of it toward the south. And you shall flee to the valley of the mountains; for the valley of the mountains shall reach unto Azal; yea, you shall flee, like as you fled from before the earthquake in the days of Uzziah king of Judah" (Zech. 14:4).

It is true that Christ ascended from the Mount of Olives, and since he will come again "in like manner" (Acts 1:11), some take this to mean he will return at his second coming to the exact spot—that his feet will touch the Mount of Olives as he faces Jerusalem. But this may be reading more into this passage than was intended. The ascension was from BETHANY (Lk. 24:50, 51), which does not overlook Jerusalem, but is on around the mount of Olives on its southeastern slope.

When we read in Zechariah 14 about a valley being formed because the mountain splits in two, we may be prone to think of this in a literal sense, and, therefore, future. But a few verses later we read: "All the land shall be turned as a PLAIN from Geba to Rimmon south of Jerusalem: and it shall be LIFTED UP, and inhabited in her place, from Benjamin's gate unto the place of the first gate, unto the corner gate, and from the tower of Hananeel unto the king's winepresses" (verse 10).

Even though actual places that were once in the area of Jerusalem are mentioned (such as the tower of Hananeel, Neh. 3:1), does anyone suppose this section of land was to be literally "lifted up" a few feet higher in elevation? This did not happen in the past, nor does it seem—if taken in a *literal* sense—very significant for the future.

BUT, figuratively, such wording about Jerusalem being exalted or lifted up, was commonly used by the prophets. Isaiah and Micah spoke of Jerusalem as a mountain being exalted above the hills (Isaiah 2; Micah 4)—words which had nothing to do with literal elevation. Words about valleys being exalted and mountains made low (Isa. 40:3, 4) were fulfilled by the ministry of John the Baptist (Lk. 3:2-5).

94

It was not uncommon for prophets to use figurative expressions about the Lord "coming" down, mountains trembling, being scattered, and hills bowing (Hab. 3:6, 10); mountains flowing down at his presence (Isa. 64:1, 3); or mountains and hills singing and trees clapping their hands (Isa. 55:12).

There are numerous Old Testament references about the Lord "coming" which cannot possibly refer to his bodily, visible second coming. Take Isaiah 19:1-4: "Behold, the Lord rideth upon a swift cloud, and shall COME into Egypt...and they shall fight every one against his brother...and the Egyptians will I give over into the hand of a cruel lord; and a fierce king shall rule over them."

In a prophecy about Jerusalem and Samaria, we read: "For, behold, the Lord COMETH forth out of his place, and will COME DOWN and tread upon the high places of the earth. And the mountains shall be molten under him, and the valleys shall be cleft" (Micah 1:3, 4). None apply this to the second coming of Christ, yet the wording is not radically different from the expressions used in Zechariah 14!

Zechariah used figurative language to describe those who opposed Zerubbabel in his work of rebuilding the temple: "Who art thou, 0 great MOUNTAIN? before Zerubbabel you shall become a PLAIN" (Zech. 4:7).

If, then, Zechariah spoke of a mountain becoming a plain, and a plain being lifted up, and numerous other figurative expressions, is it not possible that a figurative meaning could be connected with the "valley" mentioned in Zechariah 14:4?

If so, since a narrow valley could serve as a place of hiding and protection in ancient battles, it could here symbolize divine protection, a place of escape. Mention of his feet standing on the mount of Olives could have pictured his closeness and watchfulness over Jerusalem.

In another place in Zechariah, when the prophet was encouraging the returned captives in their work of rebuilding the temple, a promise of God's protection was given: "I will ENCAMP ABOUT MINE HOUSE because of the army" (Zech. 9:8). The promise of defending them was also given: "The Lord of hosts shall defend them; and they shall devour, and subdue with sling stones" (verse 15). As in other Old Testament battles, the Lord would be on their side. As they went forth fighting with primitive weapons such as "sling stones," they would be victorious. It is my opinion that such wording is best understood within an historical context when such weapons were in use.

If the expression "I am returned to Jerusalem" did not require the Lord's bodily presence after the Babylonian captivity, it is not necessarily implied that his standing on the mount of Olives, coming close to Jerusalem for its deliverance or protection, would require his visible, bodily presence either. Whether we like it or not, the prophets often spoke in figurative ways.

We believe the prophet was speaking figuratively when he said: "And it shall come to pass in that day, that the light shall not be clear, nor dark; but it shall be one day which shall be known to the Lord, not day, nor night: but it shall come to pass, that at evening time it shall be light" (Zech. 14:6, 7). If this was intended literally—that the literal sun would not set on Jerusalem—then half the world would have continual darkness, soon to degenerate into lifelessness. If the earth would cease to revolve, and the sun and moon which determine times and seasons were altered in their courses, how would men determine the date at which they would go to Jerusalem "from year to year to worship" and to "keep the feast of tabernacles"? A strict literal interpretation here has numerous problems.

On the other hand, LIGHT—understood spiritually—could refer to the truth of the gospel of Christ. Isaiah spoke of people seeing a "great light" (Isa. 9:2) which was fulfilled, according to the New Testament, by the ministry of Christ (Matt. 4:13-16). Zechariah's words about light at evening time are very similar to those of Isaiah 60:20: "Thy sun shall no more go down." Isaiah did not mean the *literal* sun, for he went on to say: "The LORD shall be thine EVERLASTING light." In the New Testament, the light that always shines, finds its fulfillment—not in the *old* city of Jerusalem—but in the *New* Jerusalem, the church! "The Lamb is the light thereof...there shall be no night there" (Rev. 21:23, 25).

Finally, one more point from Zechariah 14 should be noticed: "Living waters shall go out from Jerusalem; half of them toward the former sea, and half of them toward the hinder sea:

in summer and in winter shall it be" (Zech. 14:8). If anyone thinks this must be understood in a literal sense, he should compare Joel 3:18: "It shall come to pass in that day, that the mountains shall drop down new wine, and the hills shall flow with milk...and a fountain shall come forth of the house of the Lord, and shall water the valley of Shittim." Would any insist that literal mountains will flow with literal wine and milk?

The figurative nature of these words is also suggested by the following: Shittim was in the plains of Moab on the other side of the Jordan river (Num. 33:49; Josh. 3:1). If a literal river were to flow from Jerusalem to Shittim, it would have to cross the river Jordan to get there. *Literal* rivers flow into each other, but do not cross one another.

Jerome understood Joel's words and those of Zechariah in a spiritual sense. "A fountain will flow forth from the house of the Lord, which is the Church of Christ....Its beneficent purpose will be to change our barren land of Shittim, which yields only thorns and briars, into the fallow land of the Lord; and to refresh our dry places with copious streams; so that instead of brambles, we may yield flowers"—referring to the changes brought about by conversion to Christ.

If some feel we are wrong to "spiritualize" this verse about living waters, we need only to consider the words of Christ himself. "He that believeth on me, AS THE SCRIPTURE HATH SAID, out of his belly shall flow rivers of LIVING WATER..." (John 7:38). To what Old Testament "scripture" about "living water" did Jesus refer? Probably Zechariah 14:8! If so, he applied the passage in Zechariah—though given in the language of the Old Testament—in a spiritual way, to the living waters that flow from the body of believers, the church, the temple of God.

Many of the things we have been discussing met their FULFILLMENT within the Old Testament—Jerusalem being blessed as a center of worship, people coming there to keep the holy days, the temple being built following the Babylonian captivity, etc. Some fulfillment may have been limited because of conditions: "And this shall come to pass, IF you will diligently obey the voice of the Lord" (Zech. 6:15). And some things within these passages—though given in the wording of Old Testament vocabulary—were understood by the New

97

Testament writers as applying to Christ's spiritual kingdom, the church.

In some ways, admittedly, Zechariah is a difficult portion. But placing it in the future, and applying the literal method, does not solve these difficulties, for the following reasons:

1. If Zechariah 14 is a literal prophecy about the future, what about expressions concerning specific locations—Geba to Rimmon, Benjamin's gate, the tower of Hananeel unto the king's winepresses? These were places which pertained to Jerusalem back in the Old Testament era, but have long since been destroyed.

2. If Zechariah 14 is a literal prophecy about the future, what is now a universal worship would revert back to a localized worship at Jerusalem, men being required to go there to worship the Lord. This would be contrary to the words of Jesus (John 4:21).

3. If Zechariah 14 is a literal prophecy about the future, at the time of the second coming of Christ the nations will have gone back to primitive forms of transportation—riding horses, mules, camels, and asses (Zech. 14:15).

4. If Zechariah 14 is a literal prophecy about the future, men will again need to offer animal sacrifices (Zech. 14:21). This would be contrary to the New Testament which presents Christ as the final and perfect sacrifice for sins.

5. If Zechariah 14 is a literal prophecy about the future, then men will have to return to Judaism and keep various rituals and feast days (Zech. 14:18, 21). But according to the New Testament, these were but a *shadow* of things to come, the *substance* is found in Christ (Col. 2:16, 17). Having found the "substance," why would God require that men go back to the "shadow"? This would be exchanging the robe of Christ's righteousness for the tattered rags of Judaism!

6. If Zechariah 14 is a literal prophecy about the future—about the second coming of Christ and an age to follow—then the New Testament does not give an accurate picture of the second coming of Christ. According to the New Testament, "sudden destruction" shall come upon the wicked, "and they shall not escape" (1 Thess. 4:16-5:3). But in Zechariah, the people that fought against Jerusalem do escape. They are not all destroyed; for "every one that is left of all the nations which came against Jerusalem" would go up from year to year to keep the feast of tabernacles at Jerusalem! (Zech. 14:16). There is not the slightest hint anywhere in the New Testament that such things will follow the second coming of Christ.

JERUSALEM AND THE "LAST DAYS"

"But in the last days it shall come to pass, that the mountain of the house of the Lord shall be established in the top of the mountains, and it shall be exalted above the hills; and people shall flow unto it...the law shall go forth of Zion, and the word of the Lord from Jerusalem. And he shall judge among many people...they shall beat their swords into plowshares, and their spears into pruninghooks: nation shall not lift up a sword against nation, neither shall they learn war any more. But they shall sit every man under his vine and under his fig tree; and none shall make them afraid....For all people will walk every one in the name of his god, and we will walk in the name of the Lord our God for ever and ever" (Mic. 4:1-5; Isa. 2:1-5).

Such promises of peace and blessing were experienced at some periods within the Old Testament era. In the days of Solomon, for example, he "had peace on all sides round about him...Judah and Israel dwelt safely, *every man under his vine and under his fig tree*" (1 Kings 4:21-25). However, there are strong indications that the early Christians understood these promises as having fulfillment in the church, in the preaching of the gospel which went forth from Jerusalem, and to the peaceful conditions experienced in the lives of those who accept the gospel.

Within the prophecy, the Lord's house was to be established. In New Testament terminology, we are told that "the house of God...is the CHURCH of the living God" (1 Tim. 3:15). The church was established in power on the day of Pentecost. At that time, people "out of every nation" heard the gospel, 3,000 were converted and came into the church that day (Acts 2:5, 41). The prophecy had said that people would flow unto the house of the Lord. This has indeed been the case over the centuries during which men of all nations have been converted to Christ.

99

According to the prophecy, the word of the Lord would go forth from Jerusalem. Jesus said it was written in the prophets "that repentance and remission of sins would be preached in his name among all nations, BEGINNING AT JERUSALEM" (Lk. 24:44-47). To what passage "in the prophets" did Jesus refer? Apparently to the prophecy under consideration, given by the prophets Micah and Isaiah! If so, this prophecy was not something to take place after the SECOND coming, but was linked with the great commission given at his FIRST coming! Being endued with power from on high, those early Christians —"beginning at Jerusalem"—did indeed go forth to the nations with the word of the Lord.

If some suppose—as I did at one time—that this prophecy about the "mountain of the Lord's house being exalted" was to take place *after* the second coming of Christ, consider the TIME ELEMENT expressed. This was to happen "IN the last days"—not AFTER the last days! If the resurrection takes place "at the last day" (John 6:40, 44), then "IN the last days" would refer to a time *before* the resurrection and second coming of Christ!

Biblically speaking, the term "the last days" could certainly apply to the time of Christ's first coming, the establishment of the church, and the going forth of the gospel. And so it was used by the writer of the book of Hebrews: "God, who...spoke in time past unto the fathers by the prophets, hath in these LAST DAYS spoken unto us by his Son" (Heb. 1:1, 2).

The late C. J. Lowry, in whose church I spoke different times in Oakland, California, has written: "Correct or incorrect, the great Christian scholars, Pre-millennialists and A-millennialists of the early church, applied this prophecy to the church age. They held that Isaiah was distinguishing between the Old and the New Covenants. The kingdom of Israel under the Law conquered her enemies by the sword; the Church of Jesus Christ under the New covenant was to rebuke and conquer men by the preaching of the word and by the power of the Spirit."[36] He then cites the following examples:

TERTULLIAN spoke of this prophecy as pertaining to the new law of Christ and the universality of the gospel. As to the Lord judging among the nations, he understood this to mean those who have been called out of the nations and who, as

100

Christians, are a people of peace. In reference to that portion "they shall no more learn to fight," he said: "Who else, therefore, are understood but *we*, who, fully taught by the new law, observe these practices—the old law being obliterated." Now instead of an eye for an eye, believers in Christ are a peaceful people.[37]

IRENAEUS, writing during days of persecution, definitely applied Isaiah, chapter 2, to the church age. "But from the Lord's advent the new covenant which brings peace and the law which gives life, *has* gone forth over the whole earth, as the prophets said: 'For out of Zion shall go forth the Law, and the word of the Lord from Jerusalem; and He shall rebuke many people; and they shall break down their swords into plowshares, and their spears into pruninghooks, and they shall no longer learn to fight'."[38]

JUSTIN MARTYR wrote: "And when the spirit of prophecy speaks as predicting things that are to come to pass, He speaks in this way, 'For out of Zion shall go forth the Law, and the word of the Lord from Jerusalem, and he shall judge among the nations, and shall rebuke many people; and they shall beat their swords into plowshares, and their spears into pruninghooks: nation shall not lift up sword against nation, neither shall they learn war any more: And that *it did so come to pass*, we can convince you. For from Jerusalem there went out into the world, men, twelve in number, and these illiterate, of no ability in speaking: but by the power of God they proclaimed to every race of men that they were sent by Christ to teach to all the word of God; and we who formerly used to murder one another do not only now refrain from making war upon our enemies, but also, that we might not lie nor deceive our examiners."[39]

In another Old Testament passage, we read: "Strengthen the weak hands, and confirm the feeble knees...an highway shall be there, and a way, and it shall be called The way of holiness...the redeemed shall walk there: and the ransomed of the Lord shall return and come to Zion with songs and everlasting joy upon their heads" (Isa. 35:1-10). Here is a poetic picture of the Old Testament captives who returned from Babylonian captivity to Jerusalem. But the writer of Hebrews, takes this same passage, and applies it *spiritually!* He quotes the part about the hands and knees: "Wherefore lift up the hands which hang down, and the feeble knees"(Heb. 12:12). In verse 14, he speaks of "holiness," no doubt gleaned from Isaiah's "highway of holiness," and then, like Isaiah, he speaks about coming to Zion. "You ARE come unto mount SION, and unto the CITY OF THE LIVING GOD, the heavenly JERUSALEM, and to an innumerable company of angels, to the general assembly and CHURCH" (Heb. 12:22, 23).

When we read about coming to Zion, to the city of God, to the heavenly Jerusalem, it is evident that the *literal* city of Jerusalem is not meant. Nor does the New Testament say anything about going to Jerusalem in a future age. Such wording was intended to describe the present-tense experience of believers: "You ARE come..." The writer definitely understood Zion and Jerusalem in a spiritual sense.

The old city of Jerusalem was significant to the early Christians because of its history. It was here that Jesus ministered, was crucified, and from this area ascended into heaven. It was at Jerusalem that the disciples waited for the outpouring of the Holy Spirit. But having been blessed with this visitation, the city was now marked for judgment (Lk. 19:41-44). No longer did God's presence dwell within its temple. The New Testament writers spoke of Jerusalem as being in "bondage," as "Sodom," and "Egypt" (Gal. 4:25; Rev. 11:8). Their hopes were not in the old, literal city, but in the NEW JERUSALEM of which the old city—when at its best—was merely a type.

Chapter 12

THE NEW JERUSALEM
—Literal or Spiritual?

SOME BELIEVE THAT the Holy City described in Revelation 21 and 22 is a LITERAL city of the future. If so, it would have some very nice features. The water of this city would not be polluted. It would have pure water, clear as crystal. Instead of dusty streets (as were common when Revelation was written), it would have paved streets—paved with gold! A unique tree would provide a very healthy food for the people. The size of the city would be tremendous. It would be laid out in a square with 1,500 miles on each side. Strangely, though, it would also be 1,500 miles in height, and surrounded by a wall 216 feet high. The foundations for the wall would number 12, in which would be very fine and expensive jewels. Such is the description of the City given in the book of Revelation.

Now a city with clean water, streets of gold, and dazzling jewels would certainly be nice. We have no objection to this. However, because so much of Revelation is written in SYMBOLIC language, we should immediately question if this description was meant to be understood literally. Was John describing a literal city, or did he intend by this description to symbolize spiritual truth?

It is our belief that this description of a "city" should be understood spiritually, for an angel said to John: "Come hither, I will show you the BRIDE, the Lamb's wife." And then what happened? "He carried me away in the spirit to a great and high mountain, and showed me THAT GREAT CITY THE HOLY JERUSALEM" (Rev. 21:9, 10).

The city IS the bride of Christ, and the bride of Christ is, of course, the CHURCH. Notice Ephesians 5:25-27: "Christ also loved the Church and gave Himself up to death for her, in

103

order to make her holy, cleansing her with the baptismal water by the word, that He might present the Church to Himself a glorious *bride,* without spot or wrinkle or any other defect—holy and unblemished" (Weymouth). The word "her" (rather than "it," as in the KJV) is correct (see the context, also Moffatt, Williams, New American Standard, Phillips, NIV, Goodspeed, etc., cf. 2 Cor. 11:2).

Sometimes the church has been symbolized by a temple (Eph. 2:21), a house (Heb. 3:6), sheep (Heb. 13:20), salt (Matt. 5:13), and by other terms, none of which are taken in the literal sense. So here, the church or bride of Christ, is likened to a city complete with buildings, walls, and street. A literal city, as such, is not what will be presented to Christ as his bride, but a composite "bride" made up of *people* who know him as Lord!

The City is described as "having the GLORY of God: and her LIGHT was like unto a stone most precious, even like a jasper stone, clear as crystal...the LAMB IS THE LIGHT THEREOF" (Rev. 21:11, 23). Does the church have "the glory of God"? Certainly. "And the glory which you gave me," Jesus said, "I have given them" (John 17:22). It is "a glorious church" (Eph. 5:27). Christians have received "the light of the glorious gospel of Christ" (2 Cor. 4:4) and are "children of light" (Eph. 5:8), his "marvelous light" (1 Peter 2:9).

The WALL of the City is "great and high" (Rev. 21:12). Walls, especially important for protection in ancient times, can well symbolize God's protection for his people against the enemies of the church. Even in Old Testament poetic passages, walls were used symbolically: "And you shall call your walls Salvation, and your gates Praise...the Lord shall be unto you an everlasting light, and your God your glory" (Isa. 60:18, 19).

"And the wall of the city had TWELVE FOUNDATIONS, and in them the names of the twelve apostles of the Lamb" (Rev. 21:14). Is it not true that the church is built upon the teachings of Christ that he committed to the apostles? These 12 men took the gospel to the world. They were the founders. The church "is built upon the FOUNDATION OF THE APOSTLES and prophets, Jesus Christ being the chief corner stone" (Eph. 2:20).

"And the foundations of the wall of the City were garnished with all manner of precious stones" (Rev. 21:19, 20). Twelve stones are mentioned which correspond with the twelve stones that were in the breastplate of the high priest (Exod. 28:17-20). The symbolism here seems to be definitely rooted in this passage in Exodus.

In Revelation, 12 stones are mentioned; in Exodus there are 12 stones. In Revelation the names of the 12 apostles are in the foundations; in Exodus the 12 stones have the names of the 12 tribes. In Revelation the streets are gold; in Exodus the breastplate is decorated with gold. In Revelation the City is foursquare; in Exodus the breastplate of the high priest is foursquare.

Perhaps there is an application here to the priesthood of every believer. In Christ, all men have access to the presence of God through the gospel. Believers are called "a royal priesthood" (1 Peter 2:9) and "a kingdom of priests" (Rev. 1:6). Using precious stones to symbolize the church is not out of place, for God refers to his people as his "jewels" (Mal. 3:17).

We are told that the "City was pure GOLD, like unto clear glass...and the street of the city was pure GOLD, as it were transparent glass" (Rev. 21:18, 21). It is not uncommon for gold to be used as a symbol. Jesus said to buy "gold" (Rev. 3:18), in a setting which is obviously symbolical. The "golden candlesticks" (Rev. 1:12) are not literal candlesticks, but symbolize the seven churches (verse 20).

It is not inconsistent, then, to think of gold as a symbol—a symbol of truth. The City built of gold can symbolize the fact that the church is built with truth. Likewise, the street being pure gold can speak of absolute purity. The place upon which the saved walk is holy ground. It is the way of holiness.

Paul spoke of gold as a symbol. When men's works are tested by fire, that which is built of "gold" will stand, but the "wood, hay, and stubble" will be destroyed (1 Cor. 3:10-15). Gold, then, can well represent truth which will stand the test, the pure message of the gospel.

Adam Clarke, commenting on John's description of the city of gold, said: "This description has been most injudiciously applied to heaven; and in some public discourses, for the comfort and edification of the pious, we hear of heaven with its golden walls, golden pavements, gates of pearl, etc., not considering that nothing of this description was ever intended to be literally understood."[40]

"And the twelve gates were twelve pearls...and the GATES of it shall not be shut at all by day: for there shall be no night there" (Rev. 21:21, 25). Gates, of course, symbolize entrance into the city. The number 12 again reminds us of the 12 apostles who made it possible for men to have access into the church through their preaching. The gates are never shut, "in season and out of season," the gospel continues to be preached and men enter into the city. Since "the Lamb is the light" in this City, there is no night there. The truth of Christ continues to shine and will shine forever.

Gates facing each direction: east, west, north, and south, can speak of the UNIVERSALITY of the gospel. "And they shall come from the east, and from the west, and from the north, and from the south, and shall sit down in the kingdom of God" (Lk. 13:29).

"And he showed me a pure river of WATER of life, clear as crystal, proceeding out of the throne of God and of the Lamb" (Rev. 22:1). Spiritually speaking, what is this water which flows from God? Jesus told the woman at the well that he could give her "living water," that is, the water of life (John 4:10). In those who would receive it, this water would become "a well of water springing up into everlasting life" (John 4:14) so that from believers would "flow rivers of living water" (John 7:37, 38). This water flows from the throne of God, then through the city (the church) to the nations.

"On either side of the river, was there the tree of life, which bare twelve manner of fruits, and yielded her fruit every month: and the leaves of the tree were for the *healing of the nations*" (Rev. 22:2). As the water is called the water of life, so here the tree is the tree of life, its purpose being to provide life and healing for the nations.

There are, no doubt, portions of these two chapters (Rev. 21 and 22) which speak of the church in its final, complete, and perfect state. However, there are a number of verses which show it must be a PRESENT REALITY on earth. The water which flows in the city is available NOW. If not, what could verses like Revelation 22:17 mean: "Whosoever will, let him take the water of life freely"? Such is commonly applied to the present offer of salvation to the world.

If in the new earth there will be no sickness (spiritually or otherwise), surely the tree for life and healing must be available NOW.

Furthermore, unless the present situation is in view, how can we explain that outside the city walls "are dogs, and sorcerers, and whoremongers, and murderers, and idolaters, and whosoever loveth and maketh a lie" (Rev. 22:14, 15)? Are we to believe this is a picture of eternity—that UNHOLY things will continue just outside the walls of the HOLY city? Once we realize that the "city" symbolizes the church (which is present, as well as eternal), and that both the present and future aspects of the church are in view, all of the various parts of this passage are brought into harmony.

The city being pictured to John as coming "down from God out of HEAVEN prepared as a bride adorned for her husband" (Rev. 21:1) speaks of the heavenly, spiritual origin of the church. Coming "out of HEAVEN" is in sharp contrast to the "Beast" which comes out of the EARTH (Rev. 13:11). A strict literalism does not fit in either case.

"And the city lieth foursquare...he measured the city with a reed, twelve thousand furlongs [1,500 miles]. The length and the breadth and the height of it are equal. And he measured the wall thereof, an hundred and forty and four cubits [216 feet]" (Rev. 21:16, 17). Some have supposed that a literal city must be meant since various measurements are given. However, we must keep in mind that the city is the bride, the Lamb's wife. Therefore, such dimensions must have a symbolical meaning in relation to the church.

Take the wall, for example. When understood symbolically the wall can speak of God's spiritual protection for the church. But literally, what would be the purpose of walls 216 feet high? If this is a literal city in heaven, who are the enemies these walls are designed to keep out? Or, will the new earth "wherein dwelleth righteousness" be so wicked that walls will be needed?

Even in our time, what protection would a wall 216 feet high provide? Would such walls hinder jet planes loaded with bombs? The literal interpretation simply cannot explain any purpose for these walls. But, taken symbolically, the walls have meaning and purpose.

If the gates of pearl are the same height as the wall, these pearls would stand 216 feet high! This is the language of symbolism.

Some teach the New Jerusalem is a literal city that will come down and rest on the earth. Just how a city built 1,500 miles square—which, in size, would take up a good portion of the United States—would rest on a round earth is not explained. Or will the new earth be flat? Others believe the city will hang just above the earth like a gigantic chandelier. But if the city is to remain suspended in space, why does it have foundations? Why would it need walls?

Another problem with the literal view has to do with the height of the city—it being 1,500 miles high. Some have taught that the city is built on a high mountain, beginning at the walls with hills which gradually get higher and finally give way to a mountain which reaches this elevation. Those who hold this view apparently do not stop to reason how steep these slopes would have to be, nor do they explain what type of buildings would be built on such cliffs. The elevation of this mountain would be 7,920,000 feet (figuring 5,280 feet to a mile, multiplied by 1,500 miles). Compare this figure to that of the highest mountain in the world, Mount Everest, at a mere 29,028 feet!

The literal view has presented some strange architectural designs. Some picture this city as a huge cube, a gigantic apartment house 1,500 miles high. Figuring 10 feet to a floor, this would be 792,000 stories high! Just how desirable would it be to live in an apartment house this big?

Of course we do not doubt God's power. If such a city is indeed his plan, he can work out all details and solve all problems. But we must return to the clear statement: this "city" is the bride, the church, and therefore not a literal city (as such). Instead, these large dimensions, understood symbolically, can speak of the greatness of God's plan for his church and its ultimate perfection.

The quadrangular form speaks of its perfection and stability, for the square was anciently a figure of perfection. The square or cubical man was a man of unsullied integrity, perfect in all things. Even today, we use the expression a "square" deal, meaning one that is honest and upright. So in the symbolism here, this city is laid out in a square. But to further emphasize this perfection, it is described in three dimensions —the height being equal also!—thus forcibly expressing the concept of absolute perfection and solidity.

We might compare this description with most ordinary cities which spring up in a haphazard manner. A few streets are laid out. As a city grows, houses are built here and there and streets extended. In time, an old part of the city may be torn down to make more parking space. New shopping centers may emerge on the outskirts. Such cities—cities that grow up with little or no overall planning—have no definite shape or pattern. But the city in Revelation is described as having a definite size, measurements, pattern—all of which speaks of a PLAN.

So, the church is no last minute arrangement on the part of God. Redemption is at the very center of a perfect and unfailing plan, all of which was worked out in the divine mind even before the world began (1 Peter 1:19, 20; 2 Tim. 1:9). Surely this "great salvation," and all that is involved in it, is greater by far than a literal city with streets, walls, and gates—no matter how much gold or how many diamonds may be used to decorate it.

*   *   *   *   *   *   *   *   *   *   *   *   *   *

WE COME NOW to the closing pages of this book. We have touched on some sensitive areas. It has not been our intention to be offensive to anyone. We respect highly Christians who may hold a different view, but it is our opinion that futurism (also called dispensationalism or literalism) should be rejected.

It minimizes the fulfillment of certain prophecies in order to place them in the future. It makes the church a parenthesis in God's prophetic program, instead of the prophetic fulfillment. It must talk of a postponed kingdom and a postponed gospel. In order to hold tightly to its literalism, it would, in some instances, even have God walk backwards!

The Old Testament said that God would send Elijah the prophet. Jesus said this was fulfilled by the ministry of John the Baptist. But futurism places the coming of Elijah 2,000 years later!

According to the book of Revelation, 144,000 Israelites were to be the first converts to Christ—the firstfruits. But futurism places the time of their conversion about 2,000 years later. If this were true, it seems they should have been called the last fruits instead of the first!

Jesus said the *time* was fulfilled (at his first coming) and the kingdom was "at hand." But futurism must postpone the kingdom until 2,000 years later and make the church a mere parenthesis in the meantime.

Peter preached that the prophecy about one of David's descendants sitting on his throne was fulfilled by Christ when he ascended into heaven. But according to futurism, when Peter said this, the real fulfillment was still 2,000 years in the future!

When the Holy Spirit was outpoured on the day of Pentecost, Peter said the prophecy of Joel was being fulfilled. "This is that," he said. But according to futurism, the real fulfillment was still about 2,000 years in the future!

Even though the expression "day of the Lord" pertained to various times in Biblical history, futurism seeks to apply these scriptures to the final, end-time day of the Lord. This can only be done by minimizing the fulfillments in history, by reviving empires already gone, and by ignoring that some of these passages mentioned individuals such as Nebuchadnezzar!

To be consistent, the futurist system would require not only God to go backwards, but mankind as well. The nations would have to go back to the use of horses, ox carts, mules, and camels for transportation. Some nations, including Israel, would have to go back to ancient heathenistic forms of worship, like eating swine's flesh and mice as a religious ritual! The armies of major nations would have to go back to riding and fighting on horses, using wooden swords, spears, bows, and arrows!

The New Testament does not put fleshly Jews on a *pedestal* and the church in a *parenthesis.* Instead, all believers are *one* in Christ!

Are all Christians—regardless of race—now the sons of Abraham? Yes. "They which are of faith, the same are the sons of Abraham" (Gal. 3:7).

Are Christians—regardless of race—now the Israel of God. Yes. "...the Israel of God" (Gal.6:16).

Are Christians—regardless of race—now the circumcision? Yes. "For we are the circumcision, which worship God in the spirit" (Phil. 3:3).

Are Christians—regardless of race—now the chosen people of God? Yes. "He hath chosen us in him before the foundation of the world" (Eph. 1:4).

Are Christians—regardless of race—now a royal priesthood, an holy nation, a peculiar people? Yes. "You are...a royal priesthood, an holy nation, a peculiar people" (1 Peter 2:9).

Are Christians—regardless of race—now in Christ's kingdom? Yes. "The Father...hath delivered us...into the kingdom of his dear Son" (Col. 1:13).

Are Christians—regardless of race—now the temple of God? Yes. "You are the temple of the living God" (2 Cor. 6:16).

Are Christians—regardless of race—now called Jerusalem, the New Jerusalem? Yes. (Rev. 21:2-9).

If, then, the old Jerusalem has been superseded by the new Jerusalem, the old temple by a spiritual temple, the old priesthood by a new priesthood, the old sacrifices by the perfect sacrifice, the old circumcision by the spiritual circumcision, the old Israel by the Israel of God, why would any believe that

God will go BACKWARDS and restore the *carnal* when he has raised up the *spiritual?* Why would he go back to the *old* after having created the *new?* Why would he again recognize racial distinctions after having made all believers one in Christ? This would be RELIGION IN REVERSE!

"Divine revelation is progressive," writes Fletcher. "There is no going back, but always a going forward to something more glorious. There will never be a restoration of the 'divers washings,' 'carnal ordinances,' 'beggarly elements,' 'worldly sanctuary' with its sacrifices and Levitical priesthood, and the 'middle wall of partition' between Jew and Gentile. Such carnal, worldly, Mosaic distinctions have gone and gone forever. It seems to us that those who assert otherwise preach a revived Talmudic Judaism and ancient Rabbinism, and not the message of the New Testament."[41]

If we believe the New Testament is in the Old *contained,* and the Old is in the New *explained*—if we are willing to understand the Old Testament in the light of the New—it is clear there can be no going back. "The path of the just is as the shining light, that shineth MORE AND MORE unto the perfect day" (Prov. 4:18).

His truth is marching on!

HIS TRUTH IS MARCHING ON

Mine eyes have seen the glory
of the coming of the Lord;
He is trampling out the vintage
where the grapes of wrath are stored;
He hath loosed the fateful lightning
of His terrible swift sword,
His truth is marching on.

In the beauty of the lilies
Christ was born across the sea,
With a glory in His bosom
that transfigures you and me;
As He died to make men holy,
let us live to make men free,
While God is marching on.

Glory! glory! Hallelujah!
Glory! glory! Hallelujah!
Glory! glory! Hallelujah!
His truth is marching on.

—Julia Ward Howe (1819-1910).

NOTES

1. E. G. White, *The Great Controversy* (Mountain View, California: Pacific Press Publishing Association, original date: 1888), p. 546.

2. Albert Barnes, *Notes on Daniel* (1881), p. 344.

3. Charles T. Russell, *Studies in the Scriptures* (East Rutherford, New Jersey: Dawn Bible Students Association, 1959 edition), Vol. 2, pp. 98, 99).

4. *Ibid.,* Foreward to Volume Two.

5. William Branham, *An Exposition of the Seven Church Ages,* p. 322.

6. Charles T. Russell, *The Finished Mystery,* p. 93.

7. *Clarke's Commentary* (Nashville: Abingdon Press), Vol. 4, pp. 526-530.

8. John A. Dickson, *The New Analytical Bible* (Chicago: John A. Dickson Publishing Co., 1971), p. 1036.

9. Thomas Newton, *Dissertations on the Prophecies* (London: 1754), Vol. 2, p. 296.

10. Albert Barnes, *Barnes' Commentary.*

11. C. I. Scofield, *Scofield Reference Bible* (New York, Oxford University Press, 1917), p. 1023.

12. *The Coming of Jesus and Elijah* (Megiddo Mission, 1953), p. 28.

13. Hal Lindsey, *Late Great Planet Earth* (Grand Rapids: Zondervan Publishing House, 1970), p. 176.

14. John R. Rice, *Christ's Literal Reign on Earth* (1959), p. 12.

15. William E. Blackstone, *Jesus is Coming* (New York: Fleming H. Revell Company, 1932), p. 87.

16. Clarence Larkin, *Dispensational Truth* (1918), p. 85.

17. M.R. De Haan, *The Second Coming of Jesus,* p. 98.

18. Finis Jennings Dake, *Dake's Annotated Reference Bible* (Atlanta: Dake Bible Sales, Inc., 1963), p. 3.

19. S.D. Gordon, *Quiet Talks About Jesus* (1906), p. 114.

20. *Thayer's Greek-English Lexicon of the New Testament,* p. 356.

21. *Scofield Reference Bible,* p. 1343.

22. Harry A. Ironside, *Lamp of Prophecy,* p. 62.

23. Rice, *The Coming Kingdom of Christ* (Wheaton, IL: Sword of the Lord Publishers, 1945), p. 62.

24. Clarence Larkin, *Rightly Dividing the Word,* p. 53.

25. Herschel W. Ford, *Seven Simple Sermons on the Second Coming* (Grand Rapids: Zondervan, 1946), p. 48.

26. Dwight Pentecost, *Judgments,* p. 49.

27. *Dr. C.I. Scofield's Question Box* (Chicago: The Bible Institute Colportage Association), p. 72.

28. C. I. Scofield, *Scofield Reference Bible,* p. 1230.

29. *Ibid.,* p. 1009.

30. *Ibid.,* p. 1003.

31. Loraine Boettner, *The Millennium* (Presbyterian and Reformed, 1958), p. 244.

32. Harry A. Ironside, *The Great Parenthesis* (Grand Rapids: Zondervan, 1945), p. 106.

33. Boettner, *op. cit.,* p. 220.

34. *Clarke's Commentary,* Vol. 4, p. 533.

35. *Jerusalem, Metropolis of the Coming Age* (Christadelphian publication), p. 12.

36. Cecil J. Lowry, *Christ's Brethren* (Oakland, CA: 1955), p. 42.

37. *Ante-Nicean Fathers,* Vol. 3, p. 154.

38. *Ibid.,* Vol. 1, p. 512.

39. *Ibid.,* Vol. 1, pp. 175,176.

40. *Clarke's Commentary*, Vol. 6, p. 1060.

41. George B. Fletcher, *The Millennium—What It Is Not and What It Is!* p. 4.

By the same author...

GREAT PROPHECIES OF THE BIBLE

Will the second coming of Christ be in two stages? Will multitudes be saved after the rapture?

The "abomination of desolation"—future or fulfilled? The great tribulation of Matthew 24 —future or fulfilled? The 70th week of Daniel— future or fulfilled?

Will the Antichrist make a covenant with the Jews? A complete study on Daniel 9:27—what it says and does not say.

The "Antichrist"—Biblically linked with religious apostasy, a "falling away." What did the Reformers believe? 192 pages. Illustrated.

For a complete color catalog of books and tapes, write to:

Ralph Woodrow
Evangelistic Assn., Inc.
P.O. Box 21
Palm Springs, CA 92263-0021

R   124